# The Cycling Trivia Book

# The
# Cycling
# Trivia
# Book

### 1001 Questions from the Velocipede to Lance

## MARK RIEDY

BREAKAWAY BOOKS
HALCOTTSVILLE, NEW YORK
2008

The Cycling Trivia Book: 1001 Questions from the Velocipede to Lance

Copyright 2008 by Mark Riedy

ISBN: 978-1-891369-79-7
Library of Congress Catalog Number: 2008934824

Published by Breakaway Books
P.O. Box 24
Halcottsville, NY 12438
www.breakawaybooks.com

FIRST EDITION

# Contents

The universe of bicycles is vast. Infinite, really. So the number of trivia questions you could pose about bicycles, cyclists, and all the things they've done is infinite as well. Gathered here, though, is an arbitrary, idiosyncratic, somewhat random, and thoroughly entertaining collection of perfectly good trivia questions you can pose to yourself or to a roomful of your cycling friends. From draisiennes and velocipedes to carbon fiber and titanium; from Henri Desgrange and the Wright brothers' bike shop to Lance Armstrong, you'll find lovely bits of arcane knowledge in these pages. There's a tribe to whom such knowledge matters. People who care intensely about this elegant, incredible, life-altering machine. You know who you are.

# HISTORICAL

**True or False: The first steerable, bicycle-type vehicle had no pedals.**
True. The earliest "bicycle" was propelled by walking.

**A hobbyhorse was a bicycle that lacked what critical feature?**
A drivetrain.

**True or False: Steel is the earliest-known frame material.**
False. The first bicycle frames were made of wood.

**True or False: The pedal-powered bicycle, unveiled in 1867, was often called the Jawbreaker.**

False. Actually, it was called the Bone Shaker, because of the extremely uncomfortable ride.

**True or False: On the first true bicycles, the cranks were directly connected to the front wheel.**
True. This design brought about the large front wheels of high-wheel bicycles; these wheels allowed the rider to travel a greater distance with each revolution of the cranks.

**In the 1880s, were high-wheel bicycles more popular with the rich, or with the poor?**
The rich. The machines cost the equivalent of six months' pay for the average worker.

**Which body part was most frequently injured while riding a high-wheeler?**
The head. The combination of a high center of gravity and handlebars that also held the rider in place meant that, when the front wheel hit an obstruction such as a pothole, the rider was pitched forward onto the ground.

**In the late 1800s, what cycling organization took the lead in lobbying for better roads?**
The League of American Wheelmen, today known as the League of American Bicyclists.

When was the first pneumatic bicycle tire invented: 1875, 1888, or 1892?

1888. The first flat tire occurred a few hours later.

In 1890, a bicycle with two wheels was referred to as what?

A safety bicycle.

What event brought about the first bicycle-messenger business?

A railway strike in 1894.

True or False: Cycling was not a part of the first modern Olympic Games in 1896.

False.

In 1895, the world witnessed the first world championship competition in what cycling discipline?

Track cycling.

How many bicycles were produced in the United States in 1896?

More than one million.

What means of transportation were the first bicycles meant to replace?

Horses—a mode of travel that, unlike a bicycle, needed constant care and feeding.

**How many wheels did the first human-powered vehicle have?**
Four. The design of the human-powered carriage was first published in 1696.

**How many miles were covered in the first "long-distance" journey of a human-powered vehicle?**
12, from Paris to Versailles.

**True or False: The term *velocipede* wasn't coined until the appearance of the first drivetrain-equipped bicycle.**
False. *Velocipede*, meaning "fast foot," was the name given to the pedal-free hobbyhorse, unveiled in 1817.

**The original pedal-powered two-wheelers could sustain speeds of 6, 8, or 12 miles an hour?**
8, with only moderate exertion, which helped increase the machine's popularity.

**A pedal system—which turned the hobbyhorse into an honest-to-God bicycle—was first marketed by: A French blacksmith, an English botanist, or a German farmer?**
Pedal velocipedes were first sold along the Champs-Elysées, in the blacksmith shop of Pierre Michaux.

**How did the first bicycle manufacturer overcome the public's fear of falling?**

Michaux's company offered free riding lessons to purchasers of the bicycles.

**What was the occupation of the two bicyclists who traveled 500 miles in two weeks in the spring of 1868?**
The two were teachers, and pedaled their bicycles in France from Nice to Clermont-Ferrand—the future home of Michelin tires.

**When was the first bicycle buying guide produced?**
*Le velocipede: sa structure, ses accessoires indispensables* (*The Velocipede: its structure, its indispensable accessories*) was published in February 1868.

**What purpose did the first bicycle races, held in 1868, serve?**
They were held as a way to promote bicycle sales for Michaux et Compagnie, a bicycle manufacturer.

**When was the first women's bicycle race held?**
November 1868, in Bordeaux, France.

**When was the first patent for a bicycle filed?**
1866, in the United States. Development stalled, however, until the velocipede craze hit France in 1868.

In 1869, which magazine depicted Baby New Year arriving on a bicycle?
*Harper's Weekly.*

In 1869, this man stunned the bicycle-manufacturing community by announcing that he owned a controlling patent on bicycle manufacturing and would assess a fee of $10 on every machine sold, effective retroactively.
Calvin Witty. Surprisingly, at the time, his demands did little to slow the bicycle craze.

True or False: By the early 1870s, the bicycle craze was so pervasive that there was even a song called "The Velocipede Gallop."
True.

When did the first bicycle rentals appear?
1869. Riding academies—where new cyclists would learn the basics of bike riding—often charged money for admission, plus a per-minute charge.

What 1869 transportation event is said to have heralded the end of the first bicycle fad?
The hammering of the golden spike that completed the transcontinental railroad.

**What event halted the production of the first weekly bicycle trade journal in 1870?**
The Franco-Prussian War.

**Which country pioneered the development of the bicycle?**
France.

**In 1869, the large French bicycle manufacturer Michaux et Compagnie was renamed Compagnie Parisienne, and it adopted what English slogan?**
Time Is Money.

**One 1869 bicycle came equipped with what device to give a rider better leverage for ascending hills?**
A strap, connected to the front of the bicycle and wrapped around the back, which allowed the rider to lean backward and apply more pressure to the pedals.

**Before 1869, bicycle "tires" were largely made of what material?**
Iron.

**The first true bicycle tires were made of solid rubber. What was used to hold these first tires to the wheels: wire strands or rivets?**
Both, though manufacturers quickly developed U- and V-shaped rims to hold the tires in place.

**True or False: The first rubber tires were an immediate success.**
False. Critics dismissed the tires as a luxury that would quickly fall off the rims or simply wear out.

**The Paris-to-Rouen road race—a precursor of the Tour de France—was held in what year?**
1869. The race, which was held on November 7, featured more than 100 riders.

**When did adjustable metal spokes first appear on the market?**
1869; the British called the spoked hoops spider wheels.

**Before 1870, what was the typical size of a bicycle's front wheel?**
36 inches.

**In 1870, which technical innovation led one company to drop its intention to develop front suspension for a bicycle?**
The wire-spoked wheel.

**What was the diameter of the largest, yet still safe-to-ride, wooden wheel?**
40 inches.

**Which group of riders quickly adopted large-diameter wire-spoked wheels?**
Racers.

As front-wheel diameter grew, what did manufacturers do to keep the overall weight of bicycles in check?

They reduced the size of the rear wheel, in general to about half the size of the front wheel.

True or False: The original French bicycle company, Compagnie Parisienne, found great success well into the 1900s.

False. The company shut its doors in 1874.

Was one of the first British companies to produce bicycles originally a sewing machine manufacturer, a horse breeder, or a textile importer?

A sewing machine manufacturer: Coventry Sewing Machine Company.

True or False: In 1869, *The Lancet*, a prestigious medical journal, warned that bicycling was not suited to anyone over 40 with "diminished elasticity."

True, though it also noted that bicycling was an enjoyable means of exercise.

What was the weight of a "lightweight" bicycle in 1873?
40 pounds.

What is a common nickname for a high-wheel bicycle?
A penny farthing.

**True or False: It often took two people to get a rider onto a high-wheel bicycle.**

False. Manufacturers attached a small step on the left side of the frame; riders could stand on the step and kick the machine into motion before vaulting onto the seat and getting control of the machine.

**True or False: In 1873, the fastest riders could reach speeds of more than 25 miles per hour.**

False. Though speeds were increasing, the fastest bicycles could only travel around 20 miles per hour.

**When did the first bike club century ride take place?**

Three members of the Amateur Bicycle Club rode 100 miles in one day in 1871.

**When did individually tensioned spokes first appear on bicycle wheels?**

1874.

**By the mid-1870s, some of the first bicycle jargon was in frequent use. What was the term given to the bone-jarring, head-first crashes often taken by high-wheel bicycle riders?**

They were called croppers, as in, "He took an awful cropper."

**In 1876, David Stanton rode a high-wheel bicycle 106 miles in a single day. How long did it take him to travel the distance:**

**8.5 hours, 10 hours, or 11.5 hours?**
8.5 hours.

**In 1872, Italian riders organized the first: bicycle rodeo, charity ride, or bike-maintenance clinic?**
Charity ride. The event raised money for flood victims in Florence.

**Which American city was at the forefront of the American bicycle renaissance in the late 1870s?**
Boston

**Which American college was the first to host a bicycle club?**
Harvard, in 1879.

**What three key developments were responsible for providing the high-wheeler with its fluid feel?**
Spoked wheels with rubber tires; lightweight steel tubing; and bearings in all moving parts.

**In the late 1870s, six-day bicycle races consistently attracted large crowds. Why weren't the races held for a full week?**
Organizers wanted to keep Sunday a day of rest.

**Who described the bicycle as "an ever-saddled horse which eats nothing"?**
Albert A. Pope, founder of the Columbia Bicycle Company.

When was the first cyclometer produced?
1883, as an accessory to the high wheeler.

In 1882, the Columbia Bicycle Company was the largest bicycle manufacturer in the world. How many bikes could it produce in a single month?
1000

In 1885, a bicycle appeared that allowed what key adjustment?
The saddle could be moved up or down, forward or backward.

What piece of equipment allowed the creation of the safety bicycle?
The chain.

What moniker was given to the first "safety" bicycle to be seen as a threat to the high-wheel bicycle?
The Rover.

Among what group of people was demand for the first safety bicycles the strongest?
Women.

**What is Harriette H. Mills, of Washington, DC, best known for?**
She formed the first women's bicycle club in spring of 1888.

**The pneumatic tire was one of the greatest inventions in the history of the bicycle. But it wasn't seen as such until what important improvement occurred, three years after the tire's first introduction?**
It was made detachable in 1891, which allowed a punctured tube to be repaired in the field.

**In what year was the first shifter introduced?**
1924.

**Who said, "Everything is bicycle"?**
The author Stephen Crane.

**In 1896, what city employed the first bicycle cops?**
New York City. The five officers patrolled Central Park.

**In 1894, the International Bicycle Tournament was held at what prestigious New York City location?**
Madison Square Garden.

In 1895, what city declared, "Bloomers are not suitable for ladies' streetwear, even when worn as a bicycling costume"?
Victoria, British Columbia.

In 1895, what famous jeweler customized a Columbia bicycle that later sold for more than $3000?
Tiffany and Company. The bicycle had everything from gold-covered spoke nipples to a giant sapphire mounted to the handlebar.

Who reportedly purchased the $3,000 Tiffany/Columbia bike?
The jewel-loving Diamond Jim Brady, as a gift for the actress Lillian Russell.

In 1898, which bicycle racer held seven world records?
Marshall Walter "Major" Taylor, the first African American to become a major sports figure.

Through the 1890s, the League of American Wheelmen's membership grew to more than 100,000. But by 1902, it had fallen to what level, a sure sign that the bicycle boom was over?
10,000.

The League of American Wheelmen inspired the creation of what major association in 1902?
The American Automobile Association.

**Bicycle-maintenance skills helped craft what transportation breakthrough in the early 1900s?**
The airplane. Orville and Wilbur Wright built the Wright Flyer in their bicycle workshop.

**One of the first motorcycles was actually a bicycle powered by what?**
A steam engine.

**George Hendee, a former high-wheel bicycle racer, provided the funds to launch production of what transportation device?**
The Indian brand motorcycle.

**In the early 1900s, Ernst Sachs introduced what ride-changing device to bicycles that is still in use today?**
Freewheels, which allowed riders to keep their feet on the pedals while coasting.

**In 1902, the Raleigh Cycle Company employed Henry Sturmey and James Arches to create what labor-saving bike device?**
A three-speed hub; in 1952, production of Sturmey-Archer hubs surpassed two million a year.

**In the early 1900s, kids' bikes featured large tires and broad handlebars, and some even sported headlights, in an effort to look like what?**
Motorcycles. The bicycles often weighed 40 to 50 pounds.

Which telegraph company bought thousands of bicycles each year, and then resold them to the young messengers in its fleet?
Western Union.

If you were purchasing a kids' moto-style bicycle in 1917, which of the following would not have been an option: Luggage carrier; mudguards; headlight; tool kit; tire pump; pedals with toe clips?
Pedals with toe clips.

Which worldwide event rekindled the struggling American bicycle business in 1914?
World War I.

In what year did Frank Bowden of Raleigh Cycles say, "There is very little pleasure riding in the United States"?
1920.

What was the name of the company that launched first commercially successful rear derailleur?
Le Cyclo, which also later developed the triple chainring.

What was the cost of a fully loaded bicycle in the United States in the mid-1920s?
Around $25.

Who did Tsar Nicholas II of Russia frequently trounce on his leg-breaking rides?
His bodyguards.

How soon before the precipitous drop in bicycles sales did Albert A. Pope say, "The craze may subside a little, but I think there'll be a steady increase in the demand for cycles"?
One year.

What prompted the late 1800s to be called the golden age of illustration?
The artwork used in bicycle advertisements.

Which unlikely idea was heralded by *Cycling Life* magazine to be perhaps more important to humanity than the X-ray?
The chainless bicycle, first unveiled in 1897.

When were the first aluminum alloys used in the creation of bicycle frames?
1894. The frame was crafted by the Saint Louis Refrigerator Company.

True or False: The first derailleurs were an immediate success.
False. Several English firms developed devices to move a chain over three or four sprockets, but the idea didn't catch on for years.

In 1919, *Scientific American* featured this bicycle break-through, seen by its inventor as the next evolutionary stage of the bicycle.

A. The compact, foldable city bike created by C. H. Clark. The machine failed to garner much interest.

# GRAB BAG

**The first BMX-specific bike part was made by what company?**
Red Line Engineering, a motorcycling frame company.

**What 1971 motorcycle-racing movie sparked nationwide interest in BMX racing?**
*On Any Sunday*, which, of course, featured footage of a BMX race.

**How tall is the average BMX halfpipe?**
Between 10 and 13 feet.

What was the name of the BMX movie released in 1986?
*Rad*, starring Bill Allen.

In 1979, the first BMX freestyle team was assembled. What was the team called?
The BMX ACTION Trick Team, named after the magazine responsible for putting the team together.

Which company made the first production BMX frame?
The Webco Company.

Which company is credited with creating the first production mountain bike?
Specialized Bicycles.

Which bike is credited with sparking the BMX revolution?
The Schwinn Sting-Ray, which wasn't built for BMX but featured strong 20-inch wheels.

The movie *E.T.—The Extra-Terrestrial* featured the talents of what famous BMX name?
Bob Haro, the man behind the Haro Bicycle Corporation.

Mat Hoffman is often called the greatest vert rider in BMX history. How many tricks is Hoffman credited with creating?
At least 100.

How many presidents helmed the International Cycling Union (UCI) from its inception in 1900 through 2005?
Eight.

When were the first official Mountain Bike World Championships held?
1990.

In what year did mountain biking first appear in the Olympic Games?
1996.

Where were the first UCI-sanctioned BMX World Championships held?
Valkenswaard, Netherlands.

The year 1984 brought in the first official world championships of what well-balanced cycling discipline?
Trials.

Which bicycle suspension company's products were raced to two victories in Paris-Roubaix?
RockShox.

What's considered the standard diameter of a mountain bike wheel?
26 inches.

Are 700c wheels—the wheel size found on most road bikes—actually 700 millimeters in diameter?
No. Most road wheels actually measure closer to 680mm.

On a bicycle suspension, which adjustment controls the rate at which the suspension returns to its extended state?
Rebound.

What types of levers are used to secure the wheels (and sometimes the seatpost) to the bicycle?
Quick release.

Which material, used to make bulletproof vests, is also used in bicycle tires?
Kevlar.

In 2006, which Specialized brand bicycle celebrated its 25th anniversary?
The Stumpjumper.

What measurement is taken by measuring the distance between the center of the front wheel and the center of the rear wheel?
A bicycle's wheelbase.

True or False: The steeper the head angle, the faster a bicycle handles.
True.

**What's the name of the mechanism that moves the chain up and down the cogs on the rear of a bicycle?**
A rear derailleur.

**True or False: Most road bikes come with three front chain-rings.**
False. Most road-specific bicycles have only two front chain-rings.

**True or False: A bicycle seat is at the proper height when you can put both feet flat on the ground while in the saddle.**
False. A quick rule of thumb for setting saddle height is that your leg should only be slightly bent when at the bottom of the pedal stroke.

**True or False: Lance Armstrong has always raced on Trek bicycles.**
False.

**Super Bonus Question: Lance Armstrong was the last person to win the Tour de France using which technology?**
A. Tubular tires; B. Quill-type stem; C. Freewheel; D. Leather saddle
B. Lance was the last person to use a traditional quill-type stem (one that inserts into the fork's steerer tube as opposed to the newer stems, which clamp over the top of the steerer tube).

What do mountain bikers call a crash that sends the rider over the handlebars?

An endo.

What small, handheld tools are often used to pry clincher tires off the rim?

Tire levers.

Traditional bicycle saddles were once blamed for what male medical problem?

Erectile dysfunction.

Super Bonus Question: Name the doctor that created a solution to that medical problem.

A. Dr. Minkow; B. Dr. Strangelove; C. Dr. Bronner; D. Dr. Spock

A. Dr. Roger Minkow pioneered the medically proven Body Geometry saddle for Specialized Bicycles of Morgan Hill, California.

Who organized the first 24-hour mountain bike race?

Laird Knight.

In 1984, the first Mountain Bike Scramble was held in front of 40,000 spectators at the LA Coliseum during a motocross event. Who won the mountain bike race?

John Tomac.

In what year was the first titanium mountain bike built?
1986.

Which brand name was on that first titanium mountain bike?
Merlin Metalworks.

Who was the first American to win the Tour de France?
Greg LeMond.

Which year was it that LeMond won his first Tour?
A. 1983; B. 1984; C. 1985; D. 1986
D. 1986.

LeMond was also the first American to win which race?
A. Paris-Roubaix; B. Tour of Italy; C. Tour of Spain; D. World
Road Championships
D. Greg won the World Professional Road Championships in
1983.

True or False: LeMond also won the world championship road
race as a junior racer.
True. LeMond won the Junior World Championships in 1979.

LeMond grew up and began racing in which state?
Nevada.

True or False: LeMond was a promising freestyle snowboarder as a teen.

False. He was actually a freestyle skier.

What brand of bicycle was LeMond riding when he won his first Tour?

A. Huffy; B. Gitane; C. Bottechia; D. LeMond

B. LeMond won his first Tour aboard the French brand Gitane.

What was the name of LeMond's teammate who almost cost him the victory in the 1986 Tour?

Five-time Tour de France winner Bernard Hinault.

What event in April 1987 prevented LeMond from defending his Tour crown?

A hunting accident.

LeMond was the first big-name professional racer to embrace which technology?

A. Tubular tires; B. Shorts with synthetic chamois; C. Massage therapy; D. Wattage meter

D. Wattage meter.

True or False: LeMond was the first professional to win the Tour de France on a carbon-fiber bicycle.

True.

**LeMond was also the first racer to wear which brand of eyewear in the Tour?**
Along with select teammates, LeMond was the first professional athlete to embrace Oakley cycling optics, starting the trend of using protective eyewear in races.

**True or False: LeMond started a mountain bike team with Bob Roll as one of the riders.**
True as can be. In 1992, Roll raced for LeMond's Z Team on road and mountain.

**LeMond eventually started a bicycle company in partnership with which manufacturer?**
Trek Bicycles of Waterloo, Wisconsin

**True or False: LeMond was on the 1980 Olympic team.**
True. He was on the team, but never competed due to the boycott of the Moscow games by the United States.

**In what year was the PowerBar first introduced: 1993, 1991, or 1987?**
1987.

**Who was the sponsor of the first professional team to use the new energy food?**
7-Eleven.

Which of these three people was not one of the original inductees into the Mountain Bike Hall of Fame: Joe Murray, Neal Murdock, or Greg Herbold?
Greg Herbold.

What's the name of the original water-carrying backpack?
CamelBak.

Super Bonus Question: What was the original CamelBak reservoir based on?
As the inventor of the CamelBak was a paramedic, it's not shocking that the first CamelBak prototype used a colostomy bag.

In 1994, what percentage of all bikes sold were mountain bikes: 45%, 65%, or 85%?
65%.

Which well-known bottled-water manufacturer sponsored an all-women mountain bike team in 1994?
A. Calistoga; B. Perrier; C. Schlitz; D. Evian
D. Evian.

What is the name of the company that makes Grip Shift shifters?
SRAM.

When were Shimano's V-brakes first introduced?
1995.

What former member of the first US team to win the Giro d'Italia went on to become a bicycle announcer for the Outdoor Life Network?
Bob Roll.

Name the cycling/lifestyle brand that repopularized the use of wool as a fabric for bicycle jerseys.
Swobo of San Francisco, California.

What is the name of the small metal handlebar extensions once used by cross-country riders to provide more hand positions while riding?
Bar ends.

Because of a controversy over use of the word *freeride*, what does Rocky Mountain Bicycles call its sponsored freeriders?
Froriders.

Which company claimed legal right to the term *freeride*, triggering the "froride" controversy?
Cannondale Bicycles.

Who is often referred to as "the voice of cycling"?
Phil Liggett.

What was the name of the bike cop drama that aired for five seasons on the USA Network?
*Pacific Blue.*

Which world-champion mountain biker performed stunts on *Pacific Blue.*
Brian Lopes

How many racers were on the Discovery Channel Pro Cycling Team in 2006?
27.

What team did Lance Armstrong race for when he first won a stage of the Tour de France?
Motorola.

True or False: Before he became a professional cyclist, Lance Armstrong was a long-distance runner.
False. Lance first competed in triathlons.

Which mountain bike suspension fork is credited with jump-starting the freeride movement?
Marzocchi's Z1 Bomber.

True or False: Trek Bicycles was the first company to make a carbon fiber bicycle.
False.

How many bicycle riders are there in the United States: 30 million, 85 million, or 100 million?
85 million.

What's the name of the part of a bicycle frame extending from the bottom bracket to the rear dropout?
Chainstay.

Disc brakes come in what two distinct varieties?
Hydraulic and mechanical.

If you're a cyclist trying to ride a long distance over a set amount of time, you're competing in what?
A randonnée.

Which critical part of the bicycle connects the handlebar to the fork's steerer tube?
The stem.

True or False: Road bikes are traditionally sized in centimeters.
True.

Named after an eating utensil, this structure holds the front wheel on the bike.
The fork.

Which two bike parts are usually threaded in reverse?
The left pedal, and the right bottom bracket cup.

What's the name of the thin valves on the inner tubes often used on bicycles?
Presta valves.

Which company is credited with crafting the first modern titanium bicycle frames?
Merlin Metal Works.

What does the acronym OCLV mean when referring to the carbon-fiber construction method used by Trek Bicycles?
Optimum Compaction, Low Void.

What's the name of the major North American bike industry trade show that takes place every fall?
Interbike.

Who is Lance Armstrong's personal coach?
Chris Carmichael.

In 2006, NORBA was forced to cancel a race at Mammoth Mountain, California. Why?
Too much snow.

What name is given to a bicycle that has a single rear cog and a single chainring up front (meaning there are no derailleurs), but also allows the rider to coast?
Singlespeed.

What name is given to a bicycle that's similar to a singlespeed, except the rider can't coast—as long as the wheels are turning, the cranks are turning?
Fixed gear.

What name was given to the bikes that were the forebears of the modern mountain bikes, used to race in Repack?
Clunkers.

Which of the following is not one of IMBA's "Rules of the Trail": Plan Ahead, Leave No Trace, or Always Save Singletrack?
Always Save Singletrack.

What term is used to describe the lower, curved position of a road bike handlebar?
The drops.

True or False: On most road bikes, the brake lever and the shift lever are the same.
True.

Before the advent of integrated brake/shift levers, where were a road bike's shifters usually located?
On the down tube.

What does the acronym IMBA stand for?
International Mountain Bicycling Association.

In 2006, how much did it cost to be a member of USA Cycling?
$60.

How many miles are in a century?
100.

How many miles are in a metric century?
62.

How old should a child be before he or she rides in a bicycle trailer?
About a year old. The child should be able to hold his or her head steady while wearing a helmet.

True or False: Children's bikes are sized just like adult bikes, only smaller.
False. Children's bike sizes are based on wheel size—typically 10 inches, 12 inches, 16 inches, 20 inches, and 24 inches.

**What type of bike is otherwise known as a bicycle built for two?**
A tandem.

**Which type of bicycle offers a relaxed, legs-outstretched position, often with a highly comfortable seat?**
A recumbent.

**On a bicycle with disc brakes, what is the name of the circular piece of metal attached to the wheel's hub that works as the braking surface?**
The rotor.

**True or False: Some full-suspension mountain bikes feature 10 or more inches of rear-wheel travel.**
True.

**True or False: The term bonk refers to crashes where the rider's helmet hits the ground.**
False. It means to utterly run out of energy.

**What's the difference between an echelon and a paceline?**
In a typical paceline, the riders follow in a more or less straight line. An echelon is a variation on a paceline where the following riders are staggered to stay out of a crosswind as much as possible.

True or False: Trials bikes come in two versions: stock and modified.

True.

True or False: Ibis Bicycles founder Scot Nicol was a champion trials rider.

True.

Ibis had an innovative cable stop on some of its frames that it dubbed which of the following?

A. The Hand Job; B. The Bow Tie; The Stop Unit; Powerman 5000

A. The Hand Job was shaped like a small hand holding the end of the rear brake cable housing.

Name the Ibis full-suspension mountain bike that did not use a traditional bearing-based pivot.

The Bow Tie.

Ibis was last based in what Northern California wine country town?

Santa Rosa, California, home to American Olympic medalist Levi Leipheimer.

True or False: Component manufacturer Shimano marketed and sold a shifter that used air instead of cables to move the derailleur.

True.


In the summer of 2008, Shimano introduced which of the following?
A. Titanium crank; B. Carbon-fiber cassette; C. Electronic shifting; D. Mechanical bike shorts

C. Electronic shifting.


Italian manufacturer Campagnolo countered by offering what new product?

An 11-speed rear cassette.


At the 2005 Singlespeed World Championships, how was the final winner decided?

The top finishers (and some randomly chosen racers) competed in a go-cart race; the winner of that race won the championships.


True or False: Some early mountain bikes used road-bike-style handlebars.

True.

As of 2006, what was the maximum number of gears you could shift through on a road bike?
30.

As of 2009, what is the maximum number of gears you can shift on a road bike?
33.

What type of road bike tires need to be glued to the rim of the wheel?
Tubular tires, also known as sew-ups.

Regardless of the label on the tire, name the manufacturer behind the tubular tires on many top professionals' rims.
Dugast.

A "rigid" mountain bike lacks what comfort-increasing technology?
Suspension.

What's the name of the bike trick that's basically the same as a wheelie, except the rider doesn't pedal?
Manual.

True or False: A properly fitting helmet should move no more than an inch in any direction when you give it a good tug.
True.

True or False: A properly fitting helmet will stay on your head during a crash even if the chinstrap isn't fastened.
False.

If your child is riding in a bike trailer, should she or he still wear a helmet?
Yes.

What's the name of the tube on a bike frame that connects the head tube to the bottom bracket shell?
The down tube.

On a mountain bike, what type of jump is most often employed to get over a small obstacle?
A bunny hop.

If you balance upright on your bike without moving forward, what trick are you doing?
A trackstand.

# ROAD RACING

**What's the name typically given to the main field of riders in a race?**
Peloton. Also called a field or pack.

**Which type of road event features riders starting one after the other, racing alone over a shorter-distance course?**
Time trial.

**What's the name of the structure where track races take place?**
Velodrome.

**When a rider attempts to reach a group farther ahead, he is said to be doing what?**
Bridging the gap.

**How long is the typical criterium course?**
A mile or less.

**What construction-tool name is given to a racer who constantly pushes the pace?**
Hammer.

**What's the purpose of a lead-out man?**
A lead-out man generally "leads" the way for a teammate—usually a sprinter. The following rider drafts off the lead-out man, and is able to pull to the front and go even faster at the finish.

**A rider who refuses to take a turn at the front of a paceline and simply continues to draft off other riders is called what?**
A wheelsucker. This is not a complimentary term.

**A series of races that's held over a number of days but remains a single event—with one overall winner—is called what?**
A stage race.

**Name the American who won the 1984 Olympic road race.**
Alexi Grewal.

Can you name the rider who finished second to Grewal in a close sprint?
Canadian Steve Bauer.

Super Bonus Question: What brand of bike was Grewal on?
A Pinarello from Italy .

True or False: Grewal's bike is now in the Smithsonian Institution's National Museum of American History.
True.

What year were hardshell helmets that passed CPSC regulations mandated by the United States Cycling Federation?
1986.

How long is the track at the average velodrome?
333.33 meters.

What rider was nicknamed the Golden Boy at those 1984 Olympics?
Dana Point, California's, Steve Hegg, who won the gold medal in the individual pursuit.

What type of road race is known as "the race of truth"?
Time trial.

What's the name of the food-and-drink-filled cloth bag that riders grab during a race?

A musette.

True or False: A racer whose only job is to work to help the team leader is called a drone.

False. These hardworking riders are known as domestiques.

How much less energy does a racer use if he drafts, riding as close as possible to the racer in front of him: Up to 10% less, up to 30% less, up to 55% less?

Up to 30% less.

True or False: For registration purposes, amateur road racers are labeled beginner, intermediate, and expert.

False. Road racing uses a category system—Category 1 being elite-level and Category 5 being beginner-level.

How much does a bicycle have to weigh to be legal for UCI competitions?

At least 6.8kg, or about 15 pounds.

True or False: Mechanics have been known to put ice down the seat tube of a bicycle so that it exceeds 15 pounds when checked by officials—but the water drains out later to make for a lighter bike.

True!

**True or False: Most track racers use clipless (or click-in) pedals.**
False. Most track riders use traditional toe clips and straps for their dependable grip.

**True or False: Track riders don't believe in using carbon-fiber frames.**
False. Most top professionals now race the track on carbon-fiber frames.

**True or False: It's possible to coast (that is, ride or move forward without pedaling) on a track bike.**
False. Track bikes are fixed-gear bikes—if the rear wheel is rolling, the cranks are turning.

**True or False: Track bikes have no brakes.**
True.

**True or False: Track bikes have quick-release wheels.**
False. Quick-release hubs have traditionally been banned on track bikes because they can damage the track during a crash and because they often do not offer the same grip on the bicycle frame as a traditional threaded nut.

**What is the name of the track-racing discipline where racers are towed behind a motorcycle before being set loose for a two-lap sprint?**
Keirin.

**What are two major differences between a typical road bike and a cyclocross bike?**
A cyclocross bike is usually equipped with cantilever brakes, and with wider-than-average tires.

**According to the UCI, what's the maximum number of obstacles requiring riders to dismount that can be used on a cyclocross course?**
Four.

**True or False: All cyclocross races cover a 30-mile distance.**
False. Cyclocross races generally cover as many laps of a course as possible over a set period of time; the last lap is signaled by a bell, and the first rider to complete the bell lap is the winner.

**True or False: Cyclocross races first started as a way to attract young men to the sport of cycling.**
False. Cyclocross was originally a way for road racers to continue racing in the off-season.

**Which racing discipline is commonly called the steeplechase of biking competition?**
Cyclocross.

True or False: Cyclocross racers do multiple laps on a 5-mile track.
False. Cyclocross tracks are generally only a mile or two long.

True or False: Cyclocross racers dismount to run downhill.
False. Racers dismount to clear obstacles along the track.

True or False: Cyclocross racing is 50% riding, 50% running.
False. Regulations suggest that the split is closer to 90/10.

If you're looking at the results of a stage race, what does GC stand for?
General Classification—the overall, combined results from the multiple stages.

If you're an announcer at a bike race, how would you pronounce *prime*—would it rhyme with *lime*, or with *beam*?
With *beam*.

In most criterium races, what happens to riders who fall so far behind that the race leaders actually pass them again?
Race officials pull them from the race.

As a racer, what's the safest position in a criterium?
At the front of the pack. Accidents in the back can slow down—or bring down—following riders.

**What's another name for a one-day road race that takes place over a set loop—meaning that it starts and finishes at the same location?**
A circuit race.

**Name the three Grand Tours of cycling.**
The Tour de France, the Giro d'Italia, and the Vuelta a España.

**What are the three most contested prize competitions held in the Grand Tours?**
The individual general classification, the king of the mountains, and the points classification.

**Only two racers have won all three main prize competitions— individual general classification, king of the mountains, and points classification—at one of the Grand Tours. Who are they?**
Eddy Merckx (in the 1969 Tour de France) and Laurent Jalabert (in the 1995 Vuelta a España).

**What is the color of the overall leader's jersey in the Giro d'Italia?**
Pink.

The Giro d'Italia leader's jersey is the same color pink as:
A. The country's biggest sports newspaper; B. The former queen's favorite color; C. Italy's national color; D. The color of flesh

The country's biggest sports daily, *La Gazetta dello Sport*.

What is the color of the overall leader's jersey in the Vuelta a España?
Gold.

True or False: In cyclocross racing, it isn't unusual for the top riders to ride the same bike from start to finish.
False.

True or False: Cyclocross racers often stop for a beer during the race.
False, but it isn't uncommon for cyclocross race courses to be run through giant beer tents.

True or False: A soigneur is a type of bike mechanic.
False. Soigneurs do a variety of jobs in support of riders—from massage to organizing supplies to doing laundry—but they don't work on bikes.

Which bicycle manufacturer was most closely related to Eddy Merckx during his career?
A. Schwinn; B. Colnago; C. Peugeot; D. Lugano

B. Ernesto Colnago was Eddy Merckx's mechanic for some time and built many bikes for the star, including his legendary hour record bike.

**Which city did Eddy Merckx set his longest-lasting Hour Record in?**
A. Colorado Springs; B. Paris; C. Brussels; D. Mexico City
D. Mexico City, in 1972.

**Who was the rider who most famously broke Eddy Merckx' hour record?**
Ushering in the age of technical sophistication in bikes and training, Italian Francesco Moser broke Merckx's 12-year old record by over a kilometer.

**What sponsor is Eddy Merckx most often remembered as riding for?**
That'd be the orange and black colors of the Molteni team for which he rode from 1971 to 1976.

**Which race did Merckx not win five times or more?**
A. Tour de France; B. Paris-Roubaix; C. Milan-San Remo; D. Giro d'Italia
B. Paris-Roubaix

**Which rock star does Eddy Merckx's son share a name with?**
That'd be Axl Rose of Guns N' Roses fame.

**True or False: Merckx won more stages in the Giro d'Italia than the Tour de France.**
False. Merckx won 34 Tour stages and only 24 Giro stages.

**True or False: Merckx won the gold medal at the 1964 Olympics.**
False. He finished 12th in his only Olympic appearance.

**Today Merckx's bike company is owned by which other company?**
A. Specialized; B. Trek; C. DeRosa; D. None of these
D. Eddy still retains ownership of his brand and his company, which is based in Belgium, but sells globally.

**Which part of Merckx's body continually nagged at him during his career?**
A. His legs; B. His bum; C. His chest; D. His stomach
D. Merckx had a serious issue with his stomach that was not cleared until 2004, when he had surgery to treat the matter.

# MOUNTAIN BIKING

**What does *NORBA* stand for?**
National Off-Road Bicycle Association

**What year was NORBA created?**
A. 1970; B. 1977; C. 1983; D. 1990
C. 1983.

**Who was issued NORBA license #1?**
**A. Barbara Edelston; B. Joe Breeze; C. Gary Fisher; D. Tom Ritchey**
A. Barbara Edelston—she was NORBA secretary.

**True or False: Joe Breeze held NORBA license #2.**
True.

**Who designed the NORBA logo?**
Joe Breeze. It was used for more than 20 years.

**Who built the first modern mountain bike?**
Joe Breeze, in 1977. His Breezer was the first bike with a frame designed and built specifically for mountain biking. He used all-new parts. He took his first mountain bike immediately to the Repack downhill time trial and won.

**True or False: There was an earlier unsuccessful mountain-bike-specific frame built by Craig Mitchell for Charlie Kelly, but it was discarded after two days.**
True (sort of). The frame Charlie built actually lasted two weeks.

**What was the name of Specialized's first mountain bike?**
Launched in 1981, it was called the Stumpjumper and has been in continuous production for over 25 years.

**Who built the prototype for that first Stumpjumper?**
**Tom Ritchey; B. Tim Neenan; C. Gary Fisher; D. Gary Helfrich**
B. Tim Neenan, who was then an employee at Specialized. His name was featured on the left chainstay of the first batch of Stumpjumpers.

Gary Helfrich was part of the team that holds bragging rights to which accomplishment?

Building the first titanium mountain bike frame.

Super Bonus Question: What brand of brake levers was featured on the first edition of the Stumpjumper?

They were motorcycle brake levers from the Italian manufacturer Tommaselli.

What was the first mountain-bike-specific publication?

*Fat Tire Flyer*, published by Charlie Kelly. August/September 1980 was the first issue.

Super Bonus Question: Charlie Kelly was a roadie for what band?

Sons of Champlain.

Name the first female inducted into the Mountain Bike Hall of Fame.

Jacquie Phalen in 1988, the year it was created.

Which of the following were *not* inducted to the Mountain Bike Hall of Fame in 1988?

A. Tom Ritchey; B. Charlie Cunningham; C. Mike Sinyard; D. Scot Nicol

D. Scot Nicol. He was inducted in 1990.

### Where did Repack get its name?

After each race, mountain bikers needed to repack their coaster-brake hubs with grease—braking action on the steep downhill vaporized it into a contrail of smoke.

### True or false. Marin County rangers gained notoriety for using a radar gun to clock speeding riders on Repack and issued tickets to those that exceeded the posted speed limit of 15 miles-per-hour.

True

### True or False. Gary Fisher won the most Repack races.

False. Joe Breeze won the most with 10 out of 24 races.

### True or False: Joe Breeze now operates a company that sells bicycles primarily designed for urban transportation.

True.

### Who had the fastest time on Repack?

### A. Gary Fisher; B. Joe Breeze; C. Charlie Cunningham; D. Jacquie Phelan

A. Gary Fisher, 4:22.

### What does WOMBATS stand for?

Women's Mountain Bike and Tea Society. It was founded by Jacquie Phelan in 1984.

What was the pseudonym Jacquie Phelan's used for racing?
Alice B. Toeclips.

Where and what year did the first Marathon Mountain Bike World Championships take place?
2003 in Lugano, Switzerland.

Who were the male and female winners of the inaugural Marathon Mountain Bike World Championships?
Thomas Frischknecht (Switzerland) and 19-year-old sensation Maja Wloszcowska (Poland).

How many Elite World Championship titles did Thomas Frischknecht earn?
Two—the 1996 Mountain Bike Cross Country (Cairns, Australia) and 2003 Marathon Mountain Bike (Lugano, Switzerland).

Who crossed the finish line first at the 1996 Elite Mountain Bike Cross Country World Championships?
France's Jerome Chiotti, who later confessed to having used EPO when he won the title. As a result, second-place finisher Thomas Frischknecht was eventually awarded the rainbow jersey.

**True or False: The name of the bicycle company Gary Fisher founded in 1979 was Gary Fisher.**
False. It was originally called Mountain Bikes. He founded it with Charlie Kelly.

**What did Missy "The Missile" Giove wear around her neck during races?**
A dried piranha fish. It was her deceased pet, named Gonzo.

**How did Tinker Juarez get his nickname?**
His mom gave him the name because he was always tinkering with his bike.

**What do Juliana Furtado, Nicolas Vouilloz, and Mike King have in common?**
They all won world championship titles on a GT bike.

**What brand were Paola Pezzo's infamous golden shoes?**
Northwave.

**True or False: The first documented mountain bike race took place in Santa Cruz, California.**
False. It was held in Fairfax, California, on Mount Tamalpais and was called Repack.

What year did the first documented mountain bike race take place?
A. 1973; B. 1975; C. 1976; D. 1979
C. 1976.

Who won the first NORBA National Championships?
Joe Murray and Jacquie Phelan in 1983 (Santa Barbara, California).

True or False: John Tomac and Juli Furtado won the inaugural Mountain Bike World Championships in 1990.
False. It was Ned Overend. Tomac won the following year.

What country was Ned Overend born in?
A. Taiwan; B. France; C. the United States; D. Shredonia
A. Taiwan.

How many NORBA championships does Overend have to his name?
A. Six; B. Three; C. One; D. Five
A. Overend won championships in 1986, 1987, 1989, 1990, 1991, and 1992

Give Ned's two most popular nicknames.
'The Lung' and 'Deadly Nedly.'

True or False: Overend grew up riding on the famed trails of Mount Tamalpais in Marin County, California.

True. Ned grew up riding his road bike on the trails and fire roads when he wasn't training for cross-country running.

What year did Ned begin riding for the Specialized Bicycles team?

1988. He has ridden for Specialized ever since

What manufacturer did Ned ride for just prior to Specialized?

Schwinn.

What year did Overend move to Durango, Colorado?

April 1, 1980.

True or False: Overend moved to Durango to pursue a mountain bike racing career.

False. He moved to Durango to train at altitude for running.

Who introduced Overend to mountain biking?

"Bicycle" Bob Gregorio (who later became John Tomac's trusted mechanic) was the man who took Ned on his first fat-tire ride.

Overend won which Grand Tour?

A. The Tour de France; B. The Giro d'Italia; C. Vuelta a España; D. None

D. Ned never raced as a European road professional.

Overend won the 1990 UCI World Championships on:
A. A fully rigid Specialized; B. A Specialized Epic with a prototype RockShox fork; C. A prototype Specialized FSR full-
suspension bike; D. None of the above
B. A Specialized Epic with a prototype RockShox fork.

Speaking of RockShox, who else won their 1990 world-championship races on the prototype forks?
Greg Herbold and Juliana Furtado, respectively, won the downhill and women's cross-country events on RockShox RS-1 forks.

True or False: Rockshox founder Paul Turner grew up in Santa
Cruz, California, the company's first home.
False. Turner grew up northwest of Santa Cruz in Woodside,
California.

Based on the successful launch at the Durango World Championships, RockShox did how much in revenue in the next fis-
cal year?
A. $5000; B. $50,000; C. $500,000; D. $1.6 million
By selling only the RS-1 forks, RockShox reportedly did $1.6
million in its first real year in business.

**By 1993 what was RockShox annual revenue?**
A. $10 million; B. $15.5 million; C. $30.5 million; D. $50.5 million
C. $30.5 million.

**What was the name of RockShox's second product?**
The Mag-21.

**Super Bonus Question: What was the name of RockShox's famed Judy fork when it was still in prototype phase?**
The Diablo.

**What year did RockShox introduce its ultralightweight SID fork?**
1997.

**After Herbold's inaugural win in the world championship downhill, who was the next American to win a DH gold?**
Diamond Dave Cullinan, who was riding for Iron Horse bicycles.

**Alison Dunlap had just crossed the finish line of what event when she sank to her knees, kissing the ground?**
The 2001 Mountain Bike Cross Country World Championships, held in Vail, Colorado.

**What event did Dunlap compete in at the 1996 Olympic Games in Atlanta, Georgia?**
The women's road race.

**Who has the most world-championship gold medals for any single off-road discipline?**
That'd be French superstar Anne-Caroline Chausson, with a total of nine downhill crowns.

**Which male has the most world-championship gold medals for any single off-road discipline?**
Chausson's compatriot Nicolas Vouilloz, who took an incredible seven out of eight championships between 1995 and 2002.

**True or False: A world championship jersey for the Dual event was only awarded in 2000 and 2001?**
True!

**Which male rider won the first-ever 4-Cross event at the mountain bike world championships?**
**A. Brian Lopes; B. Eric Carter; C. Cédric Gracia; D. Wade Bootes**
A. Flyin' Brian Lopes

**Which rider won the 2008 UCI World Mountain Bike Championships aboard a prototype Specialized Epic full-suspension bicycle?**
Christoph Sauser of Switzerland won his second UCI World Championship jersey in 2008.

Which location in Switzerland was home to a mountain bike world-championship event?
A. Château-d'Oex; B. Davos; C. Crans-Montana; D. Gstaad
A. Château-d'Oex

True or false. The mother of famous wheelbuilder Steve "Gravy" Gravenites was a singer for Janis Joplin.
True

Who is Tinker Juarez's favorite movie director?
Steven Spielberg.

Cross-country mountain biking made its Olympic debut where and when?
Atlanta, Georgia, in 1996.

Who was the male 2000 NORBA overall champion?
Steve Larsen.

What was the first professional team on which famous wheelbuilder Steve "Gravy" Gravenites worked as a mechanic before making the switch to Volvo-Canondale?
Yeti, in 1986.

What company was the component sponsor for the initial Yeti squad that Gravenites wrenched for?

A. Shimano; B. SRAM; C. Campagnolo; D. Zeus

C. Campagnolo (back when they made mountain bike components)

True or False: Sven Nys won the 2007 Belgian Cross Country Mountain Bike Championships over Philippe Merenhage.

True. Roel Paulison placed third.

Before Seven Cycles, what professional mountain bike team did Olympic participant Mary McConneloug race for?

Team Jamba Juice, owned by pro racer Christine Vardaros.

What is Tinker Juarez's real first name?

David

What year did Tinker Juarez start racing bikes?

A. 1970; B. 1973; C. 1977; D. 1982

1973. He raced BMX before switching to mountain bike racing.

How old was Tinker when he became a professional mountain bike racer?

A. 16; B. 22; C. 25; D. 28

D. 28.

True or False: Tinker switched from BMX to mountain biking when Zapata Espinoza asked him to test some mountain bikes in races.
True.

Famous former Belgian mountain bike racer Peter Van Den Abeele is still working in the bicycle industry, but on the legal side. What is his new job?
UCI course inspector.

What organization founded the infamous Naked Crit—an unsanctioned criterium contested on mountain bikes held yearly at Mount Snow, Vermont?
Team Brooklyn.

True or False: The Naked Crit is completely legal because Vermont is the only state that allows full public display of nudity.
True.

Trek's 69er, a singlespeed mountain bike with 29-inch front wheel and 26-inch rear, was based on the design provided by what legendary mountain bike racer?
Travis Brown.

What was the first mountain bike manufacturer to offer a triple triangle frame design?
GT.

What was the name of the suspension design that GT launched in the late 1990s?
iDrive.

True or False: John Tomac won the overall title of NORBA World Champion.
True. He earned it in 1988. The "World" part was a misnomer, however.

What female downhill racer had a nude photo spread in *Outside* magazine's July 2000 issue? Hint: She has a tattoo on her butt cheek earned from her win at the Single Speed World Championships.
Marla Streb.

As of August 2008, how many Single Speed World Championships did Streb have to her name?
Two.

What was Streb's first year as Single Speed World Champion?
Streb won the 1999 race held in Rancho Cucamonga, California.

What about the second?
A. 2000; B. 2001; C. 2002; D. 2005
D. 2005

**Was Streb ever a Winter X Games champion for boardercross?**
No. She was the champion for downhill snow biking in 1998.

**Streb has a masters degree in which discipline?**
A. Philosophy; B. Literature; C. Physics; D. Molecular Biology
D. Molecular Biology

**Who won the 1999 NORBA cross country mountain bike race held in Mount Snow, Vermont, that Lance Armstrong entered?**
A. Lance Armstrong; B. Steve Larsen; C. Travis Brown; D. Tinker Juarez
C. Travis Brown.

**How did GT co-founder Richard Long die in 1996?**
In a motorcycle accident on his way to Big Bear Lake, California, for a NORBA National Championships Series event.

**How did GT co-founder Richard Long help finance GT Bicycles?**
With a cash settlement of several thousand dollars (along with a limp) he got from a motorcycle accident.

**Who are the two co-founders of GT?**
Richard Long and Gary Turner.

**When did GT build its first mountain bike?**
1983. The first models were called Backwoods, Timberline, and Avalanche.

**What does GT stand for?**
Gary Turner

**What mountain bike rider was sponsored by GT for longer than any other?**
A. Marc Gullickson; B. Greg Randolph; C. Juliana Furtado; D. Hans Rey
D: There's no way it's anyone other than Hans "No Way" Rey.

**What GT rider earned the nickname Chopper for his healthy sideburns?**
Greg Randolph.

**Speaking of sideburns, how did Travis Brown lose his chance to participate mountain biking's first Olympic race, held in 1996?**
He broke his collarbone pre-riding the final qualifier event held earlier that year in Traverse City, Michigan.

**True or False: Travis Brown raced in the 1990 world championships in Durango?**
True. A very young Brown took the starting line in that epic event.

**What years did Brown win the Single Speed World Championships?**
A. 1999; B. 2002; C. 2005; D. 2008
A and B

**Who won the first "modern" Single Speed World Championship?**
In an event held in Big Bear Lake, California in 1995, Adam Briggs was crowned world champion.

**From which country did the first non-American Single Speed World Champion hail?**
The United Kingdom.

**Carl Decker won the 2008 SSWC wearing what?**
A black unitard man-thong (think *Borat*), a cape, and a mask.

**True or False: Susan DeMattei was the only North American to medal at the 1996 Mountain Bike Olympics.**
False. Although DeMattei was the only US medal, Alison Sydor of Canada placed second.

**The annual Pearl Pass Klunker Tour travels between which two cities?**
Crested Butte and Aspen, Colorado.

What was the first year the Pearl Pass tour was held?
A. 1956; B. 1966; C. 1976; D. 1986
C. 1976.

What is the name of the watering hole favored by Pearl Pass riders the night before the event?
CB's Grubstake Saloon.

What is the name of the watering hole that marks the finish of the race?
The Jerome Hotel.

How many people finished that first Pearl Pass tour in 1976?
14 brave souls finished that first tour over the 12,692-foot Pearl Pass.

True or False: Gary Fisher was the winner of that first event?
False. Gary and the crew from Marin didn't show up until a few years later.

What is the name of Southern California's most infamous mountain bike club?
A. The Awesomes; B. The Rads; C. The Kooks; D. The Silver Surfers
B. The Rads.

What town do the Rads call home?
Laguna Beach.

What is the name of the Rads' biggest annual race?
The Rads Challenge.

True or False: The Rads were featured in the movie *Breakin' 2: Electric Boogaloo*
False.

Which company made the first modern clipless mountain bike pedal?
Shimano.

What is the name of another company that makes or has made a clipless mountain pedal system?
A. Burton; B. Campagnolo; C. BeBop; D. adidas
C. BeBop.

When Shimano introduced the first-ever XTR group, it had how many rear cogs?
A. 7; B. 8; C. 9; D None of the above
B. 8.

How many does it have today?
A. 7; B. 8; C. 9; D None of the above
C. 9 rear cogs.

In what year did cross-country mountain biking appear as an Olympic sport?
1996.

Which female won the women's Olympic cross-country race?
German Sabine Spitz.

In what year were the first official (UCI-sponsored) mountain bike world championships held?
1990.

Where was that first UCI mountain bike race held?
Durango, Colorado.

When did short-track racing first appear at NORBA events?
1999.

True or False: The average short-track cross-country (STXC) course is 4 miles long.
False. Most STXC courses are 1 mile or less in length.

True or False: Mountain bike races can be split into two large categories: endurance and gravity.
True.

**Where was the first organized 24-hour race held?**
Davis, West Virginia.

**True or False: Lance Armstrong once competed in a short-track cross-country race.**
True. Lance raced at Mount Snow in 1999.

**True or False: Helmets are mandatory at all mountain bike races.**
True.

**How many racers compete at one time during a mountain-cross race?**
Four.

**Are cross-country racers more likely to use bikes with front and rear suspension systems, or front suspension only?**
Front suspension only.

**What name is given to a mountain bike trail that's only about 18 inches wide, where bikers are generally forced to ride single-file?**
Singletrack.

**True or False: Professional men's cross-country mountain bike races are usually four to four and a half hours long.**
False. Most cross-country races are designed to last two to two and a half hours.

**True or False: One of the first-ever mountain bike races was a downhill race.**
True. The first Repack race was held in October 1976.

**Which event has all but replaced Dual Slalom races?**
Mountaincross.

**What race series introduced in 2006 aimed to challenge long-distance cross-country mountain bike riders with a string of 100-mile races?**
The National MTB Ultra-Endurance Series.

**Bike-mounted lights are a requirement for what kind of race?**
A 24-hour race.

**True or False: All 24-hour events are races for one- or two-person teams.**
False. These events also feature four- and five-person teams. Some have a "corporate" class that allows even larger teams.

True or False: Cross-country mountain bikes and downhill mountain bikes look almost exactly the same.
False. Downhill mountain bikes use large tires and suspension systems on both the front and back. They often look more like motorcycles than bicycles.

True or False: The amount of time a downhill racer spends on a course during a race is often less than five minutes.
True.

How many world championships did Anne-Caroline Chausson win between 1993 and 2003?
Fifteen.

If you win the Single Speed World Championships, do you receive a jersey, a plaque, or a tattoo?
A tattoo, though sometimes it's a brand.

True or False: Downhill races are mass-start events.
False. Most downhill races are run similarly to a time trial, where riders start one at a time over equally spaced intervals.

True or False: Dual Slalom and Dual races are the same thing.
False. Dual Slalom pits two riders against each other on parallel courses; in Dual races, the two tracks converge before the end, so the two racers finish on the same track.

What is the maximum number of technical-assistance areas allowed at UCI events?
Three.

When did the UCI first introduce the technical-assistance rule that allowed riders to receive parts to repair their bike at certain points in a race?
2005.

In what year was the first Dual Slalom World Cup held?
1998.

In what year did the UCI replace Dual Slalom with 4-Cross?
2002.

How many NORBA National Championships did Brian Lopes win between 1995 and 2002?
Eight.

What mountain bike race discipline is Ned Overend most famous for?
Cross-country.

True or False: John Tomac was once a professional road racer.
True.

True or False: Tomac raced for the famed 7-Eleven road team.
True

Do most cross-country racers use clipless pedals, or toe clips?
Clipless pedals.

True or False: Amateur mountain bike racers are divided into the same categories as road racers, with Category 1 being elite racers and Category 5 being beginners.
False. Amateur mountain bike racers are divided into beginner, sport, and expert classes.

Which rider is credited with launching the 24-hour solo mountain bike discipline?
John Stamstad.

Who is the only mountain biker to win the Solo World Championships six times in a row?
Chris Eatough, who won his sixth title in 2005.

Which female mountain biker won gold medals in the cross-country event at two consecutive Olympic Games?
Paola Pezzo.

In 1993, which rider earned a place in mountain bike history by collecting 17 consecutive national and international race wins?
Juliana Furtado.

Do downhill racers use full-suspension bikes, or front-suspension bikes?
Full suspension.

True or False: Mountaincross is known for its tough uphill climbs.
False. Mountaincross is a gravity event that features large jump, not climbs.

British Columbia is known as the birthplace of what style of mountain biking?
Freeriding.

# BMX

Scot Breithaupt is often called the founder of BMX. In 1970, at age 14, he organized his first BMX race. How much did racers pay to compete?
25 cents.

Did freestyle BMX riders first compete in the Extreme Games, aka the X Games, in 1991, 1995, or 1998?
1995.

In what year did the first organized BMX race take place?
1969.

In 2001, BMX racing introduced a new discipline. What was it, and during what event was it introduced?
BMX downhill was unveiled at the 2001 X Games.

A story about the 1974 Yamaha Gold Cup Series—the first large-scale BMX event—appeared in what prestigious sports magazine?
*Sports Illustrated.*

There were no BMX-specific racetracks early in the sport, so where did racers compete?
Motocross tracks. After all, *BMX* stands for "bicycle motocross."

How many racers can line up at the average BMX starting gate?
Up to eight.

When the starting gate drops at the beginning of a BMX race, racers generally go all-out in hopes of getting what early race leader's advantage?
The hole shot.

How long is the typical BMX race track?
300 to 400 meters.

Which US BMX organization, the American Bicycle Association (ABA) or the National Bicycle League (NBL), became a member of USA Cycling?
NBL.

**What's the name of the device that holds back the riders at the start of a BMX race?**
The gate.

**Which event do BMX racers simply refer to as the Grands?**
The National Bicycle League's Grand Nationals, when the National Number One titles are decided.

**Which race system is used by the American Bicycle Association?**
The transfer system, where only riders who finish first or second move on to the next races.

**Which race system is used by the National Bicycle League?**
The moto system, where riders earn points based on how they finish; the better they finish, the fewer points they receive. The racers with the fewest points move on to the next races.

**What name is given to a straight section of a BMX racetrack?**
It's called a straightaway.

**What is the name of the race category for BMX bikes with 24-inch wheels?**
Cruiser.

**True or False: BMX racing is an Olympic sport.**
True. BMX racing had its debut at the 2008 Olympics.

**Did an American win the gold in BMX at the 2008 Olympics?**
Nope. The gold was won by Maris Strombergs of Latvia. American riders took the silver and bronze.

**True or False: Long pants are mandatory at BMX races.**
True. So are helmets.

**What style of BMX competition focuses on tricks and style instead of time to the finish line?**
Freestyle.

**True or False: It's okay to race with reflectors on your BMX bike.**
False.

# RECORDS

## BMX

**In 2000, which BMX star became the first rider to complete a double backflip in competition?**
Dave Mirra.

**Who was the first American Bicycle Association National Pro Champion?**
Stompin' Stu Thomsen, who earned the title in 1979.

**Who was the first member of the American Bicycle Association BMX Hall of Fame?**
Dynamite Dave Clinton, who was inducted in 1985. Clinton is credited with creating one of the first BMX tricks, the tabletop.

**In 2003, what freestyle BMX superstar tied with skateboard legend Tony Hawk for the record number of X Games gold medals?**
Dave Mirra. Both athletes have 16 gold medals.

**In what year did Timo Pritzel and Jesús Fuentes set the record for the highest indoor BMX ramp jump?**
2001.

**How high did Timo Pritzel and Jesús Fuentes jump to set the record for the highest indoor BMX ramp jump?**
5.12 meters (16.79 feet).

**How many gyrator spins did BMX rider Sam Foakes perform in 1 minute to claim the current record?**
33.

**And, appropriately enough, where did Sam Foakes perform the BMX trick that earned him a world record?**
At the offices of The Guinness Book of World Records.

Which BMX rider set the record for highest BMX Vert Air by being towed to a 24-foot-high quarterpipe by a motorcycle?
Mat Hoffman.

What height would you need to exceed in order to set a new record for highest BMX Vert Air?
26.5 feet.

What's the highest-ever air on a BMX halfpipe?
19 feet.

Who holds the record for most BMX Pinky Squeaks?
Andreas Lindqvist of Sweden.

If you wanted to set a new record for the most continuous BMX Pinky Squeaks, how many rotations would you need to do?
At least 99, as the current record sits at 98.

How far did Mike "Rooftop" Escamilla jump to claim the title for longest BMX backflip?
62 feet, 2 inches.

True or False: When Mike "Rooftop" Escamilla jumped the longest-ever BMX backflip at X Games 11, he only won the silver medal.
False. He didn't medal at all—the jump occurred outside competition.

How many tailwhips did Romuald Noirot do to claim the record for most consecutive tailwhips performed on a BMX bike on a ramp?
Seven.

What's the distance of the longest BMX jump?
116 feet—over 13 Ford Expeditions.

BMX rider Ryan Brennan made *The Guinness Book of World Records* in 1998 for doing what at the X Games?
Being the tallest rider. He's 6 foot 6.

After landing the longest-ever BMX backflip, Mike "Rooftop" Escamilla decided to set another record. What trick did he do?
Escamilla did a 360 during a 50-foot, 6-inch jump.

In 2005, John Purse set an ABA record for the most wins in a single season. How many races did Purse win: 25, 38, or 50?
25.

# ROAD

Who was the first cyclist to break the 50-kilometer mark when setting the hour record for track cycling?
Francesco Moser, in 1984, though the UCI later changed Moser's record to "Best Human Effort" and gave the hour record time back to Eddy Merckx.

Henri Desgrange, the rider who established the hour record in 1893, is also credited with starting what cycling event?
The Tour de France.

True or False: The UCI Hour Record surpassed the 50km mark in 1995.
False. In 1995, the UCI Hour Record (not to be confused with the "Best Human Effort") remained at Eddy Merckx's 1972 distance of 49.431km.

What is the fastest recorded time for a single-person bicycle ride across the United States?
8 days, 9 hours, and 47 minutes, covering 3,107 miles, set in 1986 by Pete Penseyres.

Which famous racer held the UCI Hour Record for 28 years and 2 days?
Eddy Merckx.

True or False: Greg LeMond set the world hour record in 1991.
False. LeMond never set the world hour record

Who holds the record for the most wins of the grueling Paris-Roubaix race?
Roger De Vlaeminck of Belgium.

How many times did Roger De Vlaeminck win Paris-Roubaix?
Four.

What amount of time separated first and second place in the closest Tour de France in history?
8 seconds.

Who won the Tour de France by only 8 seconds?
Greg LeMond, in 1989. Second place went to Laurent Fignon.

Many said that Fignon's what cost him the race?
A. Eating habits; B. Late-night partying; C. Tire choice; D. Ponytail
D. Ponytail!

To beat Fignon, LeMond pioneered the use of which technology?
A. Clincher tires; B. Aero handlebars; C. Skin suits; D. EPO
B. Aero handlebars.

Name the "inventor" of the aerobars used by Lemond.
Boone Lennon.

Lennon worked with which cycling brand to develop the aerobar into a product that any cyclist could buy at a local shop?
Scott USA.

What sport did Boone Lennon come to cycling from?
Alpine skiing.

Lennon would later go on to create a system for learning which sport?
A. Skiing; B. Cycling; C. Snowboarding; D. Scuba diving
C. Lennon created the Quick Carve snowboarding learning system.

Where did Felicia Ballanger win the world record for the fastest 500-meter women's cycling race?
Bogotá, Colombia.

What time would you need to beat if you wanted to claim the world record for the fastest 500-meter women's cycling race?
34.017 seconds.

True or False: Lance Armstrong's last Tour de France was also his fastest.
True. Lance's average speed was 25.882 mph.

The 2005 Tour de France was the fastest ever. How long did it take Lance Armstrong to complete the 2,241-mile race?
86 hours, 15 minutes, and 2 seconds.

**Which Italian rider holds the record for the fastest average speed in a Tour de France stage?**
Mario Cipollini.

**As extravagant as they come, Cipollini was fined for what?**
Wearing non-official team jerseys during the Tour de France, most notably skin suits inspired by the movie *Tron* that featured the human anatomy, and a tiger print.

**Cipollini holds the record for winning the most stages in which event?**
A. Tour of Italy; B. Tour of Spain; C. Tour of France; D. Tour of America
Cipollini has the record for winning 42 stages of the Tour of Italy.

**Cipollini won the World Professional Road Racing Championship in which year?**
A. 1985; B. 1995; C. 2002; D. 2005
C. 2002, in Zolder, Belgium.

**After a brief retirement, Super Mario Cipollini came back to race with which professional team?**
USA-based Rock Racing.

In track racing, what nationality is the record holder for the fastest men's 200-meter flying-start sprint (as of fall 2008)?
Canadian.

How long did it take Curtis Harnett to cover 200 meters to claim the record in the 200-meter flying-start sprint?
9.865 seconds.

During what major 1996 sporting event did track racer Florian Rousseau set the record for the fastest 1-kilometer sprint from a standing start?
The Olympic Games in Atlanta, Georgia.

What time would you need to beat in order to claim the title of the fastest 1-kilometer sprint from a standing start?
1 minute, 2.712 seconds.

As of 2002, was the world-record time for cycling 200 miles on a track: just under 8.5 hours, 10.5 hours, or 14 hours?
Just under 8.5 hours. The actual time was 8 hours, 29 minutes, 32 seconds.

Was the record for the greatest distance ridden in 12 hours, solo and unpaced, set on the Lehigh Valley Velodrome in Trexlertown, Pennsylvania; Novo Mesto Velodrome in Novo Mesto, Slovenia; or the Bellville Velodrome in Cape Town, South Africa?

Novo Mesto Velodrome in Novo Mesto, Slovenia.

**How far did Marko Baloh pedal to set the record for the greatest distance ridden in 12 hours on a track, solo and unpaced?**
452.196 kilometers (280.9 miles).

**How many cyclists can claim to have won seven Amateur World Cycling Championship titles?**
Two.

**True or False: One of the cyclists to have won seven amateur World Cycling Championship titles is an American.**
False.

**What's the largest number of Olympic medals to be won by a single cyclist?**
Five.

**When did Daniel Morelon win his first Olympic cycling medal, on his way to becoming the cyclist to win the most Olympic medals?**
1964.

**Between 1977 and 1986, how many World Cycling Championship titles did Koichi Nakano win in the pro sprint event?**
10.

Who is the only cyclist ever paid *not* to compete in the Giro d'Italia?
Alfredo Binda.

How many cyclists have won the Giro d'Italia five times?
Three: Alfredo Binda, Fausto Coppi, and Eddy Merckx.

How many cyclists have won the Giro d'Italia only three times?
Five. Giovanni Brunero, Gino Bartali, Fiorenzo Magni, Bernard Hinault, and Felice Gimondi.

Italian Gino Bartali won what Giro d'Italia title a record seven times?
King of the Mountains.

Who are the only two riders to have won the Vuelta a España a record three times?
Tony Rominger and Roberto Heras.

How many world championship titles has Jeanne Longo won in her career?
Twelve.

In 1996, how many miles did Michael Secrest ride in 24 hours to set a new world record?
532.74.

# MOUNTAIN

Which racer has won a record number of world championships, Brian Lopes or Anne-Caroline Chausson?
Chausson.

True or False: Chausson won the first-ever women's Olympic BMX event in 2008.
True. American Jill Kinter took the bronze medal.

Who is the only mountain biker to win the 24 Hour World Championships six times in a row?
Chris Eatough.

Who won the first official Repack mountain bike race in 1976?
Alan Bonds.

Which French mountain biker holds the record for the fastest speed down a glacier?
Christian Taillefer.

What speed would you need to beat in order to claim the title of "fastest cyclist on snow"?
132 mph.

Aside from unveiling the first production mountain bike, Specialized Bicycles is also known as the first major bicycle manufacturer to produce what?
A website.

How old was Emmanuel Gentinetta when he set the record for mountain biking the Pan-American Highway from Alaska to Argentina?
18. It took him 261 days to travel 15,233.98 miles—Gentinetta even traveled to Antarctica to set his record.

Who is the only mountain biker to win both a cross-country and a downhill world championship?
Juliana Furtado.

When she retired in 1997, Juli Furtado held the record for all-time World Cup cross-country victories. How many races did she win?
28.

In 2000, trials rider Ryan Leech set an unofficial world-record height with what jump?
The sidehop.

How high was the bar that Ryan Leech cleared to set the unofficial world record?
106cm (41.7 inches).

Which former Race Across America winner holds the current winter trans-Alaska time record for mountain biking 1,049 miles from Anchorage to Nome?
Bob Fourney.

What's the current time record for biking from Anchorage to Nome, Alaska, in winter?
14 days, 7 hours, and 40 minutes.

In 2004, distance racer Mike Curiak set a record by racing from Canada to Mexico along what 2,490-mile route?
The Great Divide Mountain Bike Route.

How long did it take Mike Curiak to ride from Canada to Mexico during a 2004 race?
16 days and 57 seconds.

In 1995, John Stamstad set a record for the most miles ridden on a mountain bike in a 24-hour period. How many miles did he ride?
354.64 miles.

French mountain biker Nicolas Vouilloz won an astonishing 10 world championships in what cycling discipline?
Downhill.

Which rider was given a Guinness world record for the most X Games medals in snow mountain biking: Brian Lopes, Cheri Elliot, or Sabrina Jonnier?
Cheri Elliot.

Which famous mountain bike dirt jumper became the first to ride a full loop on his mountain bike?
John Cowan.

Which two riders won the first-ever Olympic gold medals in cross-country mountain biking?
Paola Pezzo of Italy, and Bart Brentjens of the Netherlands.

Which now retired racer nearly became the first male racer to win a world championship in both cross-country and downhill in the same year, but ended up winning the silver medal in the DH?
John Tomac.

What type of rear wheel did Tomac frequently use?
A Tioga Tension Disc.

Which crash-prone mountain biker once earned a world record for landing a 41-foot cliff drop?
Josh Bender.

The 2006 running of the Kokopelli Trail Race saw a new course record set—on a singlespeed mountain bike. How long did it take the winner to complete the 140-mile race?
13 hours and 26 minutes.

In 2003, a new course record was set for Colorado's Grand Loop race. How long did it take the winner to finish the approximately 360-mile event?
3 days, 2 hours, 37 minutes.

In the fall of 2003, the New England Mountain Bike Association became the first mountain bike advocacy group to do what?
Purchase and own property. The group bought and now manages the 47-acre parcel that local riders call "Vietnam."

# MISCELLANEOUS

If you wanted to set a world record for riding backward on a bicycle, how far would you have to pedal?
More than 113.3km in 6 hours.

And what if you added a violin?
Then you'd only have to travel more than 60.45km in 5 hours and 9 minutes.

On February 2, 2006, Jason Rennie jumped his Kona mountain bike a world-record distance. How far did he fly?
133 feet, 6 inches.

What is the fastest speed ever achieved on a bicycle?
167.043 mph.

Where did Fred Rompelberg ride his bike when he set the record for the highest speed ever achieved on a bicycle: the Luis Carlos Galán Velodrome in Bogotá, Colombia; the Bonneville Salt Flats in Utah; or Mount Washington, New Hampshire?
The Bonneville Salt Flats, Utah.

True or False: When setting the record for fastest speed ever on a bicycle, Fred Rompelberg did not draft behind a car.
False.

What was the diameter of the rear wheel of the smallest bicycle ever ridden?
0.51 inch.

How far did electrician Zbigniew Rozanek, of Poland, ride the world's smallest ridable bicycle?
16 feet.

How long is the longest bicycle?
92 feet, 2 inches—and it really only has two wheels.

Over how great a distance did the engineering students who built the world's longest bicycle actually manage to ride the bike?
328 feet.

What is the front-wheel diameter of Frankencycle, the world's largest bicycle?
10 feet.

True or False: The oldest woman ever (she lived 122 years and 164 days) was still riding a bicycle at 120.
False, although she did ride well into her 100s.

Where did Xavi Casas claim his record for most stairs climbed by a bicycle?

The Eiffel Tower.

How many steps did Xavi Casas climb to claim the record for most stairs climbed by bike?

1,374.

What's the largest number of possible gear combinations ever put on a single bicycle: 30, 48, or 1,500?

1,500. ·

In 1999, Kurt Osborn rode a bicycle from Hollywood, California, to Orlando, Florida, which in itself isn't a record. What did Osborn do to get this journey into the record books?

He rode a wheelie the whole way—meaning he balanced on his rear wheel and pedaled 2,839.6 miles.

How tall is the world's tallest bicycle: Just over 12 feet; just over 18 feet; or just over 25 feet?
Just over 18 feet—18 feet, 2.5 inches tall.

How far did Terry Goertzen pedal the world's tallest bicycle to make it into *The Guinness Book of World Records*?
1,000 feet.

In 2000, Steve Stevens decided to pedal a penny farthing (that's a high-wheeler) across the United States—and he set the record for such a crossing at the same time. How long did the journey take?
29 days, 9 hours, and 3 minutes.

# HUMAN PERFORMANCE

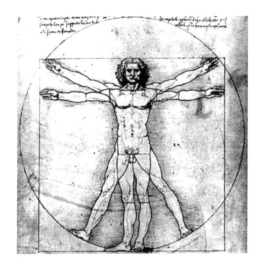

True or False: Most high-end bicycling power measurement devices measure a cyclist's output in horsepower.

False. Most measure power output in watts.

According to Lance Armstrong's personal coach, how many watts could Lance generate when he was in top Tour de France form?

Close to 500.

How many watts will the average recreational cyclist generate and sustain during an hour-long bike ride?
About 150 watts.

Theoretically, is it better for cyclists to have long or short femurs?
Long. Longer femurs improve leverage.

The equation "220 – (your age)" can provide what useful piece of training information?
Your maximum heart rate.

True or False: The lower your resting heart rate, the more fit you are.
True.

True or False: Stiff-soled cycling shoes can help prevent numbness in the feet while riding.
True.

True or False: A study conducted by a University of Texas at Austin researcher concluded that bicycling helped increase sexual arousal in women.
True.

What term is used to describe the maximum amount of oxygen, in milliliters, a cyclist can use in one minute per kilogram of body weight?
$VO_2$ max.

True or False: The more fit you are, the lower your $VO_2$ max.
False.

True or False: Pedaling at a higher velocity (high rpm) reduces the amount of force required for each pedal stroke.
True.

Which of these three former Tour de France champions had the highest $VO_2$ max: Miguel Indurain, Greg LeMond, or Lance Armstrong?
Greg LeMond.

At the pre-race medical check for the 2005 Tour de France, 2 riders had the lowest resting heart rate of the 189-rider field. Was that heart rate 20 beats per minute, 35 beats per minute, or 42 beats per minute?
35 beats per minute.

Which rider had the greater lung capacity at the start of the 2005 Tour de France, Lance Armstrong or Christophe Moreau?
Christophe Moreau.

When a cyclist's foot is at the bottom of the pedal stroke, should the angle of the knee be closer to 30 degrees, 45 degrees, or 65 degrees?
30 degrees.

True or False: With the cranks level (that is, with the feet in the three o'clock and nine o'clock positions), the kneecap should sit in front of the toes.
False. The knee shouldn't pass beyond the ball of the foot.

A 1996 study of recreational cyclists who had just completed a long-distance bike tour found that what percentage of the riders suffered from knee pain: 45%, 55%, or 65%?
65%.

True or False: If you develop pain behind your knee, it could be a sign that your saddle is too high.
True.

If you ride with aerobars—the clip-on armrest-type extensions favored by time trialists and triathletes—what's the ideal angle between your shoulder and upper arm when you ride on the bars?
90 degrees, so that your elbows are under your shoulders.

For a recreational road cyclist who is riding with his or her hands on the brake hoods, what should be the angle between the rider's upper body and the bike's top tube?
45 degrees.

If a road cyclist is riding in the handlebar's drops, what's the ideal angle between his or her torso and the bike's top tube?
30 degrees.

True or False: You can use an inseam measurement to get a rough estimate of what size road bike you should ride.
True. Multiply your inseam measurement in inches by 2.54, then multiply that number by 0.67.

Over the course of a 24-hour race, how many calories will 24 Hour World Solo Champion Chris Eatough ingest to fuel his effort: 7,000; 10,000; 15,000?
15,000.

Anatomically shaped saddles are designed to relieve pressure on what critical blood-delivering arteries?
The pudendal arteries.

Cyclists who place too much pressure on their hands for long periods of time can cause numbness in their ring and pinky fingers by compressing what nerve?
The ulnar nerve.

For cyclists, which upper-body part is most frequently injured in a fall?
The shoulder.

A cyclist riding with his or her hands in the drops is using which muscles to the fullest effect?
The gluteus muscles.

True or False: Cycling is a high-impact sport.
False.

True or False: A proper-fitting bike will put you in the same body position used by most pro cyclists.
False.

When using clipless pedals and properly set cleats, what part of the foot does the pedal axle cross while riding?
The ball of the foot.

How many calories will a 176-pound man burn while riding at a recreational speed for one hour: 350, 480, or 650?
About 480.

When adjusting a bike for ideal fit, a plumb line dropped from the front of the knee while sitting on the bike, when the pedals are level, will align with what part of the bike?
The front of the crankarm.

True or False: On a proper-fitting bike, the saddle should be angled downward slightly.
False. The saddle should be level with the ground.

Reach is a combination of what two measurements?
Top-tube length and stem length.

In general, the width of your handlebars should equal: the width of your shoulders, or the measurement from your elbow to the tip of your middle finger?
The width of your shoulders, measured between the acromio-clavicular joints.

True or False: Sprinters and criterium racers often use too-narrow handlebars.
True. The narrower width lets them squeeze into narrow openings.

True or False: Women riders often use wider handlebars for greater steering stability.
False.

To prevent numbness while riding on the brake hoods, they should be positioned so that your hands feel like they're performing what common greeting?
A handshake.

Which hand position is considered the default position for road riding: riding with your hands in the drops, on the top of the bars, or on the brake hoods?
On the brake hoods.

To alleviate "hot foot"—burning pain in the ball of the foot during long rides—should you move the cleats farther forward, or farther to the rear of the shoe?
To the rear.

What term is used to describe a natural, resting foot position where the ball of the foot is higher than the outside of the foot?
Forefoot varus.

Approximately how many pedal strokes will the average rider make during a 6-hour century ride: 28,600; 32,400; or 50,100?
32,400 (pedaling at 90 rpm for 6 hours).

True or False: If you raise your saddle, you should raise your stem the same amount.
True.

Riding with bare knees in cold temperatures can lead to injury. Most experts recommend covering the knees with knee warmers or tights if the temperature drops below what level?
65 degrees F.

To warm up sufficiently at the start of a ride, you should spin easily for how long: 5 minutes, 8 minutes, 15 minutes?
15 minutes.

True or False: The faster your pedaling cadence, the harder it is on your knees.
False.

In order to give your body time to adapt to your training loads, you should increase your mileage each week by no more than: 5%, 10%, or 20%?
10%.

What device is used for adjustment if a rider has one leg that's longer than the other?
A shim.

Unless a rider is suffering from back pain, most fit experts won't adjust for a leg-length discrepancy unless the difference is greater than: 6mm; 1cm; or 1.5cm?
6mm. If back pain is involved, however, that measurement drops to 3mm.

During the 1983 Race Across America, Michael Shermer gave his name to the malady "Shermer neck." What is it?
Extreme neck fatigue—the neck muscles become so weak that they can no longer support the weight of the head.

What custom piece of equipment did the first American Tour de France champion use to alleviate his extreme discomfort on the bike?
LeMond used custom shoes.

What's one of the most common mistakes riders make when it comes to their bike shorts?
They wear underwear beneath their shorts.

True or False: Overtraining is a strictly physical condition.
False. There's often a psychological component as well.

Which of the following is not a symptom of overtraining: Sudden weight loss, decreased resting heart rate, or depression?
Decreased resting heart rate.

William Morgan, MD, who pioneered research on overtraining, once said, "I haven't seen an overtrained athlete who wasn't clinically _____": Underweight, depressed, or addicted to exercise?
Depressed.

How many calories are typically burned during 1 hour of hard training or racing?
Approximately 1,000.

**What famous Winston Churchill advice is often followed by professional racers at rest?**
Never stand when you can sit, never sit when you can lie down.

**Professional male racers often have body fat percentages around: 5%; 8%; or 12%?**
5%.

**If a rider loses 1 pound of body weight, how much does his performance improve on a hilly course?**
About 1%.

**As a rule of thumb, cycling burns approximately how many calories per mile: 25, 40, or 55?**
40.

**What name is given to the point where the body can no longer process lactate as quickly as it is produced?**
Lactate threshold, or anaerobic threshold.

**Endurance performance is often predicted by taking what measurement at a rider's lactate threshold?**
Power output in watts.

**True or False: Taller riders should use longer crankarms.**
False.

True or False: The foot only pushes directly down on the pedal at the three o'clock position.
True.

True or False: A slow pedaling cadence requires a larger muscular force.
True.

True or False: Pedaling at a high rpm places less effort on the muscles and more on the cardiovascular system.
True.

Force-measuring pedals have allowed researchers to discover what about pulling up on the pedals during the pedal stroke?
That almost no riders exert any real upward force on the pedals.

Which riders have a smoother pedal stroke, road racers or cross-country mountain bikers?
Mountain bikers.

Greg LeMond once described the ideal pedal stroke as feeling like what?
Scraping mud off your shoe at the bottom of the pedal stroke.

Do sprinters have more fast-twitch or slow twitch muscle fibers?
Fast twitch.

Hypoglycemia (low blood sugar) can make you feel light-headed, weak, confused, and tired. What term do cyclists generally use to refer to this problem?
Bonk.

The term *glycogen window* refers to a period after exercise where the body is especially adept at replenishing glycogen from food. Generally speaking, how long is this window thought to be open?
Up to four hours.

How many gallons of liquid will 24 Hour Solo World Champion Chris Eatough ingest over the course of a race: 3, 5, or 10?
5.

How many liters of air does the average cyclist breathe in per minute?
4.

When an athlete's body runs out of carbohydrate to burn and switches to burning fat, energy output is limited to what percentage of $VO_2$ max: 90%, 75%, or 50%?
50%.

Approximately how many calories does the body store as glycogen: 1,000; 1,500; or 2,200?
1,500.

Early season "base" training often refers to what type of riding?
Easy-speed, high-mileage riding.

How many weeks of base training should most cyclists aim for at the start of each season?
At least eight.

In addition to improving aerobic conditioning, build training works to improve what?
Muscular strength and power.

True or False: Most lactate-threshold rides are more than an hour in length.
False.

True or False: Tempo rides are performed at a moderately hard exertion level.
True.

Does the peaking period of a cyclist's training plan generally include the event being trained for?
No. The peaking period focuses on short, intense training.

True or False: Most top athletes can only do two days of quality training each week.
True.

True or False: You can increase your power at LT by doing intervals slightly above your LT pace.
True.

How many calories will the average cyclist burn on a century ride?
4,000.

True or False: Pre-ride stretching is extremely important.
False. Better to stretch once you're warmed up.

True or False: One of the easiest recovery techniques is to elevate your legs after a ride.
True.

True or False: Goal-oriented riders are more likely to overtrain.
True.

True or False: After an all-out effort, a female cyclist's buildup of lactic acid is usually lower than a male's.
True.

True or False: Recent studies have concluded that caffeine can help reduce thigh muscle pain during exercise.
True—good news for all the espresso-loving cyclists out there.

When were the first scientifically tested, anatomically friendly cutout bicycle seats introduced?
1999.

Which manufacturer introduced that first saddle?
Specialized Bicycles of Morgan Hill, California.

What was the name of that first anatomically correct saddle?
The Specialized Body Geometry saddle

While riding, is it better for most riders to focus on having their knees closer to the top tube, or farther away?
Neither. The knee, hip, and foot should all be in line.

True or False: If your feet are larger than a size 9 (men's), you'll be more efficient by moving your pedal cleats farther back on your cycling shoes.
True.

Aside from aerodynamics, what benefits do cyclists reap by wearing Lycra shorts?
The snug, form fitting shorts can help reduce muscle fatigue and boost performance.

Which muscles contribute more to a cyclist's ability to attack climbs, his arms or his lower back?

Lower back. It's why Tyler Hamilton was able to finish the 2003 Tour de France with a broken collarbone, but had to drop out of the 2004 Tour when he bruised his lower back in a crash.

How many liters of blood will the average 30-year-old cyclist's heart pump in one hour if he's working at 80% of his maximum heart rate: 450, 525, or 638?

638.

True or False: Although a woman's muscle strength is about two-thirds that of a man's, there's less of a discrepancy in leg strength than in upper-body strength.

True.

True or False: A straightedge placed against the bottom edge of a drop handlebar can help determine the lowest position at which the brake levers should be set.

True. The tip of the brake lever should just touch the straight-edge—the levers shouldn't be set any lower than this.

If a highly trained cyclist stops exercising altogether, how long would it take to lose half his or her aerobic conditioning: Three weeks, six weeks, or three months?

Three months.

# TECHNOLOGY

**What diameter is commonly considered the standard for a bicycle's steerer tube?**
1 1/8 inches

**Which mountain bike suspension company was the first to create suspension forks to match the OnePointFive standard?**
Manitou.

**In the early 1990s, which bicycle company produced bicycles using the 1¼-inch-diameter "Evolution" steerer-tube size?**
Gary Fisher Bicycles.

In 2006, a third company started selling complete bicycle drive-trains to the public. What was the name of that company?
SRAM.

Which two companies were the first to offer complete bicycle drivetrains?
Campagnolo and Shimano.

Which component company was the first to offer a 10-speed drivetrain to the public?
Campagnolo.

What was the name of the Shimano shifting system that used compressed air to shift the rear derailleur?
Airlines.

What type of riding was Shimano's compressed-air shift system designed for?
Downhill mountain biking.

When you're talking about Mavic's UST wheels, what does UST stand for?
Universal System Tubeless.

True or False: A guy named Stan created a way for regular mountain bike tires to be run without tubes.
True.

How many sides do the Crank Brothers Eggbeater pedals have?
Four.

What does the *R* stand for in Shimano XTR?
Racing.

What gas is commonly used as a shield when welding titanium?
Argon.

Most "anatomically friendly" bicycle saddles sport what feature?
A hole to ease pressure on the perineum.

What shape are the spokes in a wheel that's meant to be highly aerodynamic?
Flat, or bladed.

To reduce the harsh ride of aluminum bicycle frames, some manufacturers are producing road bikes that use what material for the seat and/or chainstays?
Carbon fiber.

What feature on a full-suspension mountain bike shock helps control unwanted movement from pedaling forces?
A platform.

**What is the difference between a singlespeed bike and a fixed-gear bike?**
A singlespeed bike has only one gear, but you can coast. A fixed-gear bike has one gear that's directly connected to the rear wheel—if the wheel is turning, the pedals are moving.

**What type of damping controls the rate at which a suspension mountain bike returns to the "normal" position after absorbing a bump?**
Rebound.

**If the spokes on a wheel go straight from the hub to the rim without overlapping another spoke along the way, the wheel is said to be laced how?**
Radially.

**Unless they fall into the "Small, Medium, and Large" category, mountain bike frames are measured in inches. How are road bike frames measured?**
Centimeters.

**A disc brake that is activated by a cable—meaning that a brake cable runs from the brake lever to the caliper—is called what kind of brake?**
Mechanical.

True or False: Disc brakes are UCI-legal on cyclocross bikes.
False. But you can still buy them with disc brakes.

True or False: Specialized's FSR suspension was originally developed by Mert Lawwill.
False. It was developed by Horst Leitner.

True or False: Doug Bradbury is the founder of RockShox.
False. RockShox was founded by Paul Turner.

Cable housing—the sheath that covers brake and shift cables—is made up of plastic-coated metal. With traditional brake housing, does the inner metal run the length of the housing in individual strands, or is it wrapped in a spiral?
Wrapped in a spiral.

Which company first introduced compressionless cable housing?
Shimano.

Should compressionless housing be used as brake-cable housing, or shift-cable housing?
Shift-cable housing.

What is the name of the small metal cap that fits over the end of a piece of cable housing?
A ferrule.

How are tubular tires held to a bicycle wheel?
With glue.

Modern suspension forks typically use either coil or air springs. Early on, however, another spring type was common. What were those springs made of?
Elastomer. (Basically, they were rubber bumpers.)

What does an SRM Powermeter measure?
A cyclist's power output in watts.

What are the two types of fluid that can be used in hydraulic disc brakes (though not at the same time)?
Mineral oil and DOT brake fluid.

What is the diameter of the handlebar clamp if the handlebar is an "OS" bar?
31.8mm.

What does the acronym *VPP* stand for?
Virtual Pivot Point.

What bicycle tool company's trademark color is blue?
Park Tool USA.

If you pick up a bicycle tool with a yellow and black handle, there's a good chance it's made by this company.
Pedro's.

How long is the warranty on Chris King headsets?
10 years.

True or False: To shift using Grip Shift shifters, you push a lever with your fingers.
False.

Typically speaking, if you're on a ride and you puncture your tubeless tire, what can you do to reinflate the tire and continue riding?
Install a tube.

What are the two main ingredients used to create a carbon-fiber bicycle frame?
Carbon fibers and epoxy.

Calfee Designs uses what type of wood in one of its frame designs?
Bamboo.

What did Mavic's Mektronic shifting system use to activate shifts?
Electricity.

Most road bike shifters use two levers to shift—one to move the derailleur up, the other to move it down. How many levers are used by SRAM's road shifters?
One.

Are modern bottom bracket bearings found inside the bottom bracket, or alongside the bottom bracket?
Alongside.

What gear ratio is a good starting point for a singlespeed bike?
2:1. For example, a 32-tooth chainring and a 16-tooth cog.

True or False: It's possible to shift between chainrings while using a chainguide.
True. You just need the right type of chainguide.

True or False: Cyclocross bikes have road-bike-like frames, but use different brakes than road bikes.
True.

What size Torx wrench do you use if your disc brake rotor is held on with Torx bolts?
T-25.

Shimano's Center-Lock hubs let you use what tool to install a disc brake rotor?
A cassette lockring tool.

**Suspension forks and shocks typically use one of two spring mediums. What are they?**
Air or metal coil.

**How do "compact geometry" road bikes differ from "standard" road bikes?**
Generally, they have a radically sloping top tube and shorter seat tube; a longer-than-usual seatpost puts the rider in the proper position.

**What's another name for tubular tires?**
Sew-ups.

**What kind of wrench do you use to tighten bolts that put clamping force on carbon-fiber parts?**
A torque wrench.

**What was the moniker given to the elliptical mountain bike chainrings (said to increase efficiency and power transfer) first produced by Shimano in the 1980s?**
BioPace.

**Lights are mandatory equipment for 24-hour races; an HID light is one type of light that many racers use. What does *HID* stand for?**
High-intensity discharge.

**What was the name of the first company to produce a hydration pack?**
CamelBak.

**If you use a wet lube on your chain, how often should it be applied?**
Before every ride . . . or whenever you remember to do it.

**What type of stem is used with a threaded headset?**
A quill stem.

**What does *SPD* stand for?**
Shimano Pedaling Dynamics.

**Why are clipless pedals called clipless pedals if the cleat on your shoe still clips into the pedal?**
It's a holdover from when the pedals first came out and started replacing the old toe-clip-and-strap pedal system.

**Why should you use bike-specific cable cutters when cutting cables and housing?**
You're less likely to fray the cable or mash the end of the housing.

**Which is worse for your helmet: Leaving it in the closet for a year, or leaving it in the backseat of your car for a week?**
Unless your closet has a skylight, the backseat of your car. The sun's UV rays can wreak havoc with the foam in your helmet.

Which type of valve, found on some bicycle tubes, matches the valve found on a car tire?
A Schrader valve.

What part of the tire holds the tire to the rim?
The bead.

If your rear brake lever pulls uncomfortably close to the bar and you want to tighten it back up (and improve your braking), do you turn the brake's barrel adjuster clockwise, or counterclockwise?
Counterclockwise.

What would be one valid reason for mountain bikers to wear baggy shorts, if it were true?
Added protection in case of a fall.

When the shift cable enters the rear derailleur, it often does so in an exaggerated loop—why?
The straighter the cable enters the derailleur, the less friction there will be.

Which bicycle company is famous for its use of Celeste green?
Bianchi.

A minimum of how many lugs is used to build the typical dia-mond-shaped lugged frame?
Four.

In a lugged frame, how are the tubes joined?
Brazing, usually with silver or brass.

True or False: Aluminum is the most common frame material today.
True.

What's the common spacing for a road bike's rear dropouts?
130mm.

What's another name for a hex wrench?
Allen wrench.

True or False: If your seatpost tends to slip in your frame, roughing it up with sandpaper could help.
True.

What part of the wheel does a derailleur-hanger-alignment tool use as a guide for straightness?
The rim. So make sure it's true.

How is a Shimano E-type front derailleur attached to the bike?
It mounts to the bottom bracket, and is held in place by the right-side bottom-bracket cup.

True or False: To quickly gauge the correct length of a mountain bike chain, you wrap the chain around the big chainring and big cog, overlap by one link, then remove the excess links and install the chain.
True.

True or False: If you're on a ride and slice open a tire, you can seal the hole by placing a dollar bill inside the tire (over the hole, of course).
True.

When tightening a threadless headset, do you first tighten the steerer-tube-clamp bolts on the stem, or the topcap bolt?
The topcap bolt.

True or False: If the teeth on your chainring are shaped like little shark fins, it's time to replace the chainring.
True.

Of what material are Brooks saddles typically made?
Leather.

**What purpose do bar ends serve?**
They provide more leverage for climbing, as well as a more stretched-out position for smooth roads. Or, none. It depends on whom you ask.

**True or False: To remove an old quill-type stem, you often have to loosen the top bolt, then strike the bolt with a mallet or hammer.**
True.

**SRAM is best known for what type of shifting system?**
Grip Shift.

**SRAM's parent company owns what other brand(s)?**
**A. Zipp; B. Avid; C. RockShox; D. All of the above**
D. All of the above.

**Name SRAM's longtime sponsored racer and field tester.**
Greg Herbold.

**True or False: A sealed bearing is basically waterproof.**
False. Sealed bearings do a better job at keeping stuff out, but they aren't watertight.

**True or False: A chainwhip is used to remove a stuck chain.**
False. It's used to hold a cassette so the lockring holding the cassette in place can be removed.

True or False: A road bike with a shorter wheelbase will handle more quickly.

True.

What material are Campagnolo's Record level shifters made of?

Carbon fiber.

What type of crank interface do most high-end bottom brackets use: Square-taper, or splined?

Splined.

What's the most accurate at-home method for determining saddle setback?

With the pedals level, drop a plumb line from the front of the knee; it should touch the end of the crankarm.

What's the name of the device that can measure various body angles (knee angle, hip angle) to help determine proper bike fit?

A goniometer.

True or False: The larger the disc brake rotor, the greater the brake's potential stopping power.

True.

Name the two mounting standards for disc brake calipers.
International Standard (or A-type) and Post-Type.

Touring bikes are often made of what easy-to-repair-in-far-flung-destinations material?
Steel.

True or False: A stretched-out position can be detrimental on long climbs.
False, though it can make for sketchy descending.

Which mountain bike fork is said to have helped start the freeride movement?
The Marzocchi Z1.

Which mountain bike suspension design was resurrected by Santa Cruz Bicycles in 2002?
Virtual Pivot Point, or VPP.

What bike company first developed the VPP design?
Outland.

Which bicycle company made a brief foray into motor sports, producing quads and motocross bikes for a few years before reverting to a bicycle-only company?
Cannondale.

# LANCE ARMSTRONG

## TOUR DE FRANCE

Armstrong won how many consecutive Tours de France?
Seven

True or False. Lance Armstrong was the first US rider to win the Tour de France.
False. Greg LeMond won it in 1986, 1989, and 1990.

True or False: Armstrong was just 25 when he won his first Tour de France.
False. He was 27 years old when he won his first in 1999.

What was Armstrong's typical weight at the start of one of his seven Tour victories?

A. 150 pounds; B. 160 pounds; C. 165 pounds; D. 175 pounds

C. 165 pounds.

In which year's Tour did Armstrong win his first stage?

A. 1993; B. 1997; C. 1999; D. 2005

A. Stage 8 in the 1993 Tour de France.

How many Tour de France stage wins did Armstrong have during his career?

A. 20;  B. 22; C. 15; D. 7

B. 22.

When did Armstrong win his first Tour de France yellow jersey?

The 1999 prologue—his first day of returning to the Tour post-cancer.

What was the greatest number of stage wins Armstrong had in any one overall Tour de France victory?

In the 2004 Tour de France, Armstrong won five stages and his Discovery team won the team time trial.

Which rider finished second to Armstrong in his first Tour victory in 1999?

Swiss star Alex Zulle.

How many times did Jan Ullrich finish on the final podium in a Tour won by Armstrong?
Four times: 2000, 2001, 2003, and 2005.

Armstrong's signature stage win in the 1999 Tour finished in what Italian Alpine village?
Sestriere.

What was Armstrong's last stage victory in the Tour de France?
The Stage 20 individual time trial in 2005; fittingly, Jan Ullrich finished second on the day.

Why was it especially important for Armstrong to win the 1995 Tour de France Limoges stage?
So he could dedicate it to his teammate Fabio Casartelli, who died earlier in the Tour on the Portet d'Aspet descent.

When Fabio Casartelli had the deadly crash on the Portet d'Aspet descent, what rider crashed with him?
A. Lance Armstrong; B. Richard Virenque; C. Giuseppe Guerini; D. Johan Museeuw
D. Johan Museeuw

On what Tour de France climb did Armstrong give "the look" to Jan Ullrich?
Alpe d'Huez in 2001.

True or False: In 2003, Armstrong had his fifth overall Tour win in the 100th year of the Tour de France.
True.

What Tour de France climb was Armstrong attacking when his handlebar was swiped by a yellow supporter bag?
Luz Ardiden.

Who was also taken down by the unfortunate yellow supporter bag incident?
Iban Mayo.

True or False: Armstrong won four stages in the 2004 Tour de France.
False. He won five.

What was Armstrong's favorite hotel to stay in the night after capping off a Tour victory in Paris?
The Hotel de Crillion just off the Place de la Concorde.

What notable event first happened in the 2004 Tour? Hint: It involves Times Square.
Armstrong's victory in the Alpe d'Huez time trial was shown on a giant screen in Times Square—the first time the Tour was shown live there.

Name the only person to be Armstrong's teammate for all

seven Tour victories.
George Hincapie.

How many times did Armstrong win the stage that finishes on top of Mont Ventoux?
A. Zero; B. One; C. Two; D. Three
A. Zero. Armstrong had some great rides of "The Giant of Provence" but was never able to win this grand stage.

What brand of coffee was Armstrong's chosen fuel during his reign as Tour champion? Hint: It's from the San Francisco Bay Area.
Peet's Coffee

In the 2003 Tour de France, what fallen cyclist was Armstrong trying to avoid when he performed his memorable cyclocross maneuver?
Joseba Beloki. It took place in the town of Gap.

True or False: Tour de France television commentator Bob Roll was once a Tour de France teammate of Armstrong's.
False! Although both raced for the Motorola team, Armstrong and Roll were never teammates.

On July 13, 2000 Armstrong was accused of disrespecting Marco Pantani by not sprinting him for the win at what mountain top finish?  A. Mont Ventoux B. Alpe d'Huez C. Col du

Tourmalet D. Col d' Aspin

A. Mont Ventoux

What race did Armstrong use the most frequently as a final tune-up for the Tour de France? A. Tour of California; B. Tour of Spain; C. Tour of Italy; D. Critérium du Dauphiné Libéré

D. Armstrong rode the Critérium du Dauphiné Libéré before five of his seven Tour victories.

True or False: The main sponsor of Armstrong's team for six of his seven Tour victories was the United Parcel Service.

False. It was the United States Postal Service.

What brand of bicycle did Armstrong ride for all seven of his Tour de France victories?

Armstrong rode a bicycle from Waterloo, Wisconsin-based Trek Bicycle for all of his Tour victories.

When did Armstrong publicly announce that he was going to try for Tour de France win number seven? A. February 12, 2005 B. March 31, 2005 C. April 18, 2005 D. May 15, 2005

C. April 18, 2005

What was the name of the ex-professional cyclist who directed Armstrong's team for all seven of his Tour de France victories?

Belgian Johan Bruyneel was Armstrong's directeur sportif for all of his Tour victories

# CANCER

In what year was Armstrong diagnosed with cancer?
A.1994; B. 1995; C. 1996; D. 1997
C. 1996.

His odds of beating the testicular cancer that he had been diagnosed with were?
A. 50/50; B. 20/80; C. 80/20; D. 90/10
A. 50/50.

How many days after Armstrong's cancer diagnosis did he undergo his first surgery?
A. The same day; B. One day; C. Two days; D. Three days
B. One day.

Armstrong underwent chemotherapy in which town?
A. Austin; B. New York; C. Louisville; D. Indianapolis
D. Indianapolis.

True or False: In addition to chemotherapy, Armstrong underwent two operations to fight the spread of testicular cancer.
True.

How much estimated weight did lance lose over the duration of his Chemotherapy sessions?
A. 10 pounds; B. 20 pounds; C. 30 pounds; D. 40 pounds
B. 20 pounds—he lost it during four cycles, three weeks each, of chemotherapy.

What famous former professional cyclist came to Texas to do a time trial with Lance Armstrong during his recovery from cancer?
Eddy Merckx.

For what team did Lance Armstrong race when he announced he had cancer?
Cofidis.

In what year did Armstrong found the Lance Armstrong Foundation to fight cancer?
1997.

Armstrong memorialized the date of his diagnosis by naming his Nike clothing line after it. What is that date?
2/14; B. 6/15; C. 9/11; D. 10/2
D. 10/2.
When was Armstrong's last chemotherapy session?
A. February 1997 B. May 1997 C. November 1997 D. March 1998
C. November 13, 1997

Armstrong and Nike released the now iconic yellow Livestrong bracelet in what year?
2004.

By 2005, how many Livestrong bracelets had been sold?
A. 10 million; B. 1 million; C. 200,000; D. 55 million
D. 55 million.

True or False: Armstrong served on the President's Cancer Panel under President George W. Bush.
True.

True or False: The Lance Armstrong Foundation's signature fund-raising event is the Livestrong Challenge.
True.

# MISCELLANEOUS LANCE

**Armstrong was the honorary starter for which event?**
A. The Indianapolis 500; B. The Kentucky Derby; C. The New York Marathon; D. The Tour de France
A. The Indianapolis 500.

**In 2008, Armstrong opened a bike shop in Austin, Texas, named what?**
A. Mellow Johnny's; B. Armstrong Cycles; C. Austin Bikes; D. Lance's
A. Mellow Johnny's.

**His shop specializes in selling what kind of bikes?**
Commuter bikes.

**Armstrong appeared in which movie?**
A. *Superbad;* B. *Gladiator;* C. *You, Me and Dupree;* D. *The Royal Tenenbaums*
C. *You, Me and Dupree* in 2006.

True or False: In 2007, 36-year-old Armstrong was romantically linked to 21-year-old Ashley Olsen.

True.

True or False: In 2007 Armstrong went on a USO tour with Venus Williams.

False. He did a USO Tour, but with Robin Williams.

In 2006, Armstrong and which famous rock musician broke off their engagement?

Sheryl Crow.

In 2006, what did Armstrong do for the first time?
A. Eat ice cream; B. Ride a mountain bike; C. Race an Ironman; D. Run a marathon

D. Run a marathon—the New York Marathon in this case.

Armstrong was on the board of which hotel chain?

Morgans.

After retiring, Armstrong led which tour?

RAGBRAI—The *Register*'s Great Annual Bike Ride Across Iowa

Armstrong was frequently shown in gossip magazines hanging out with which superstar friend?
A. Matthew McConaughey; B. Tiger Woods; C. Ozzy Osbourne; D. Steve Jobs
A. Matthew McConaughey.

Which "capital" University did Armstrong receive an honorary degree from?
The George Washington University

Which national fitness center chain opened 'Lance Armstrong' branded fitness centers after his retirement?
24 Hour Fitness.

In 2005, Armstrong hosted which famous weekly television show?
A. 60 Minutes; B. Saturday Night Live; C. Meet the Press; D. Survivor
B. Saturday Night Live.

Armstrong was the honorary captain for which football team?
The University of Texas Longhorns.

True or False: In 2006, Armstrong said actor Jake Gyllenhaal was going to be cast to play him in a movie about his life.
True.

True or False: Armstrong is named after former Dallas Cowboys receiver Lance Rentzel.

Apparently, this one is True. Rentzel played for Dallas in the 1960s and '70s.

Armstrong hosted which awards show in 2006?
A. The Oscars; B. The Grammy Awards; C. The MTV Movie Awards; D. ESPN's ESPY Awards.

D. ESPN's ESPY Awards

How many ESPY Awards has Armstrong received in his lifetime?

Six.

True or False: Scientists named a planet after Armstrong.

False. It was actually an asteroid—1994 JE9 was named 12373 Lancearmstrong in honor of the seven-time Tour winner.

The United States Postal Service Pro Cycling Team presented by Berry Floor operated during what years?

1996-2004.

Annie Lebowitz is the photographer responsible for the impressionist nude photo of Armstrong on a bike.

False. Her name is Annie Leibovitz.

**True or False: In 2008, Armstrong won the Leadville Trail 100 race.**
False! Armstrong was beaten by longtime Colorado mountain bike racer and six-time Leadville winner David Wiens.

**Other than New York, in what city did Armstrong plan to race a marathon in 2008?**
Chicago.

**What is Lance Armstrong's favorite football team?**
Dallas Cowboys.

**In March 2008, Armstrong dropped $20,000 on what piece of art from the Scope Art Fair at New York's Lincoln Center?**
**A. Wooden sculpture of a naked woman with erect nipples; B. Pixel image of a bike; C. Abstract painting of Monaco countryside; D. Tiffany lamp**
A. Wooden sculpture of a naked woman with erect nipples by Richmond, Virginia, artist Morgan Herrin. In addition, the sculpture was holding a sword, and what looks like an octopus obscured most of her face except her lips.

**After what event did Armstrong comment, "Nothing in the Tour de France compares to this. It was much harder than I expected. It's only a two-hour race, but it was the hardest two hours of my life."**
After the 1999 Mount Snow NORBA mountain bike race.

True or False: Lance Armstrong had his drink removed by a bouncer at the Fourth Street Bar in Austin, Texas, as he tried to exit with it. Armstrong's retaliation included the quip, "You'll never work at this bar again."
True. Shortly after, Armstrong admitted he was out of line.

How old was Armstrong when he became World Champion?
A. 20 B. 21 C. 22 D. 23
B. 21

True or False: Armstrong said, "Pain is temporary. It may last a minute, or an hour, or a day, or a year, but eventually it will subside and something else will take its place. If I quit, however, the pain still goes away."
False. The correct quote ends with, "If I quit, however, it lasts forever."

What is the name of Lance Armstrong Foundation fund-raising ride?
Ride for the Roses.

When Armstrong was looking for a new team, who was the guy at US Postal Service who believed in his successful return to racing?
Mark Gorski.

What was Armstrong's first major UCI win after his post-cancer return to racing?
Tour of Luxembourg, 1998.

What is Lance Armstrong's original last name?
A. Armstrong; B. Edwards; C. Gunderson; D. Billows
C. Gunderson.

What is Lance Armstrong's middle name?
Edward.

How many times was Armstrong's mother married and divorced?
A. Two; B. Three; C. Four; D. Five
C. Four.

When Armstrong and Sheryl Crow met at the Grand Slam for Children event in Las Vegas, October 2003, what was their main flirting device?
The BlackBerry.

True or False: Armstrong proposed to Crow in the middle of a lake on a small fishing boat that ran out of gas.
True. Far from feeling stranded, Lance seized the perfect moment to propose.

What was the carat size of the engagement ring Armstrong gave to Crow?
A. Three; B. Four; C. Five; D. Six
D. Six-carat, cushion-cut.

In 2007, Lance Armstrong was a co-founder of Athletes for Hope, a charitable organization that helps pro athletes get involved in charitable causes. Which of these athletes was *not* a co-founder?
A. Tiger Woods; B. Andre Agassi; C. Muhammad Ali; D. Cal Ripken, Jr.
A. Tiger Woods. The other founders were Warrick Dunn, Jeff Gordon, Mia Hamm, Tony Hawk, Andrea Jaeger, Jackie Joyner-Kersee, Mario Lemieux, and Alonzo Mourning.

What is Lance Armstrong's resting heart rate?
A. 28-30 bpm; B. 32-34 bpm; C. 36-38bpm; D. 38-40bpm
B. 32-34 bpm.

In 2006, Armstrong was the pace car driver of a Chevrolet Corvette Z06 at what major event?
Indianapolis 500.

True or False: President George W. Bush invited Armstrong to his Prairie Chapel Ranch to go for a road ride.
False. He was invited to go for a mountain bike ride.

**True or False: Armstrong has won the Amstel Gold Classic.**
False. His best placing was second.

**What was the name of Lance and Kristin Armstrong's first child, born in October 1999?**
Luke David.

**True or False: When Lance Armstrong won the world championships in 1993, he crashed two times.**
True.

**When Armstrong started his athletic pursuits, in what sport did he first show promise?**
Swimming.

**In what year(s) did Armstrong become National Sprint Triathon Champion?**
A. 1988-1990; B. 1989-1990; C. 1987-1989; D. He was never National Spint Triathlon Champion
B. 1989-1990.

**What is Armstrong's favorite chamois cream?**
Assos Chamois Cream.

**What are Armstrong's twins names?**
Isabel and Grace.

Where did Armstrong's cross necklace come from?
A. Former wife Kristin; B. His mother; C. Eddy Merckx; D. Stacy Pounds (Armstrong's agent's administrative assistant)
D. Stacy Pounds asked Armstrong to wear it before she died of lung cancer in 1997.

In addition to the cross, what other pendant is on Armstrong's necklace?
The state of Texas. He used to have a tiny heart from former wife Kristin, but it fell off.

In 2007, Armstrong dated which fashion designer for a few months?
Tory Burch, creator of a women's sportswear and accessories lifestyle collection.

True or False: In 2008 Armstrong was sued by someone that made Barkstrong dog collars.
This one is unfortunately True!

Armstrong was the youngest rider to win which race?
The World Professional Road Racing Championships

Armstrong's first professional victory was in which race?
Stage 6 of Italy's Settimana Bergamasca

**What year was Lance Armstrong born?**
**1964; B. 1974; C. 1975; D. 1971**
D. September 18, 1971.

**Armstrong's first love was which sport?**
A. Soccer; B. Swimming; C. Triathlon; D. Rollerblading
C. Triathlon.

**Armstrong's mother's first name is?**
Linda.

**Lance Armstrong is from which town in Texas?**
A. Austin; B. Plano; C. Dallas; D. Paris
B. Plano.

# BIKE CULTURE

What brand of bicycle usually hung on Jerry Seinfeld's wall?
Klein.

And what brand bike replaced it for one episode?
A. Never replaced; B. Specialized; C. Trek; D. Cannondale
D. Cannondale.

In *E.T.—The Extra-Terrestrial* (1982), what brand of bicycle was used by Elliott to carry E.T. in the basket while flying in front of the moon?
A. Schwinn; B. Redline; C. Kuwahara; D. Huffy
C. Kuwahara (aka Kuwie). It is a Japanese bicycle company. Schwinn opted not to be involved with the movie production.

For how many people was the longest tandem built?
A. 7; B. 15; C. 22; D. 35
D. 35. It was almost 67 feet long and weighed about as much as a Volkswagen.

True or False: The smallest bicycle that an adult can ride is equipped with wheels made from silver dollars.
True.

In 2007, what was the name of the documentary movie on the San Francisco messenger or fixie scene?
A. *Stomp*; B. *Fixed*; C. *Mash*; D. *Slap*
C. *Mash*.

How many stories high is the tallest functional unicycle?
A. 3; B. 5; C. 7; D. 10
D. 10 stories tall, built and ridden by Steve McPeak. He claims the greatest challenge was not in riding the machine, but in building it so that the chains would not fall off the sprockets.

What was the name of the first vegetarian professional cycling team created in 2000?
Linda McCartney Racing Team.

Wilbur and Orville's Wright's bicycle company, The Wright Cycle Company (formerly Wright Cycle Exchange), was founded in what year?
A. 1852; B. 1888; C. 1893; D. 1910
C. 1893 in Dayton, Ohio.

The bicycle that won Calfee Design multiple awards at the North American Handmade Bicycle Show was made out of what material?
Bamboo.

Cyclocross is referred to as *Veldrijden* in Belgium. What is this word's literal translation?
Field riding.

What sport is President George W. Bush fanatical about?
Mountain biking.

What beloved Muppet was seen on camera for the first time in full (below the waist) while riding a bicycle?
Kermit the Frog in Jim Henson's *The Muppet Movie* (1979). Kermit was headed for Hollywood.

**What eventually happened to this beloved Muppet's bike?**
It was squashed by a steamroller.

**True or False: The first two-wheeled rider-propelled machine was called the Laufmaschine.**
True. It was also called the draisienne. It was invented by Baron Karl von Drais de Sauerbrun of Germany. In 1817, he rode it for 14 km (9 miles), and the following year he exhibited it in Paris.

**What is the bike most commonly used by bike messengers?**
Fixed-gear bike

**Buster Keaton's *Our Hospitality* (1924) includes a great scene with Stoneface riding what type of bike?**
Draisienne (Laufmaschine)

**In the movie *Quicksilver* (1986), what bicycle did Jack Casey (Kevin Bacon) use for the entire movie?**
One-speed 1984 Raleigh Competition.

**What variation was made to Jack Casey's bike in *Quicksilver*? A. Made into a fixed gear; B. Outfitted with zero-degree angle trick forks; C. Equipped with a BMX freewheel; D. All of these**
D. All of these.

**What American Olympic medalist was featured in the opening scene of *Quicksilver*?**
How about Nelson "The Cheetah" Vails, silver medalist and former bicycle messenger.

**The 2008 national conventions of both the Democratic and Republican parties shared what?**
A fleet of 1,000 bikes provided by the not-for-profit Bikes Belong

**The 1985 movie *American Flyers* starred which 1980s heartthrob? A. Tom Cruise; B. Kevin Costner; C. Burt Reynolds; D. Dom DeLuise**
B. Kevin Costner.

**In *American Flyers*, Costner's character Muzzin's nickname is "the Cannibal." He shares his nickname with what famous cyclist who also appears in the film?**
Eddie Merckx, five-time Tour de France champion.

**The dog that chases *American Flyers* star Kevin Costner while he's out training is nicknamed what?**
**A. Cannibal; B. Eddie; C. Tiger; D. Psycho**
B. Eddie

The movie also features the daughter of what sky-high 1970s comedian?
Rae Dawn Chong, daughter of Tommy Chong, was featured in the film.

True or False: Cycle polo is officially recognized by the UCI (International Cycling Union).
True—since 2001

In *American Flyers,* what is the actual location of the race held at the fictitious "Monumental National Park"?
Colorado National Monument, located west of Grand Junction.

In *American Flyers,* what team did Muzzin ride for?
A. Team Brooklyn; B. Motorola; C. 7-Eleven; D. Molteni
7-Eleven. The actual professional 7-Eleven Team became Team Motorola in the early 1990s.

True or False: There exists a form of competitive indoor cycling in which athletes perform ballet/gymnastic-style tricks on bikes.
True. It is called artistic cycling.

"Bill felt the first touch of breeze on his bald pate and his grin widened. *I made that breeze,* he thought. *I made it by pumping these damn pedals.*" This quote is taken from what popular novel?
*It* by Stephen King. The book was made into a movie in 1990.

True or False: In the movie *2 Minutes* (1998), Laurie gives up bike racing and finds refuge in being a bike messenger.
False. It was called *2 Seconds*.

In the animated film *Les Triplettes de Belleville* (2003), what is the name of the orphaned boy who is raised by his grandmother to be a professional bike racer?
A. Pierre; B. Orphan Boy; C. Michel; D. Champion
D. Champion

After seeing *Breaking Away* (1979), you'll never be able to eat zucchini or linguini without thinking of Raymond Stoller (Paul Dooley)'s tirade against what kind of food?
"-ini" food.

In *Breaking Away*, what was the name of the famous race on the track, and what university held it?
The Little 500, put on by Indiana University. Held since 1951, it is the largest collegiate bike race in the United States.

### Who starred in the 1934 movie *6 Day Rider?*
Joe E. Brown. He appeared in over 70 films and was best known for his role *in Some Like It Hot* (1959), where he played wolfish millionaire Osgood Fielding III.

During a beautiful scene in the movie *Il Postino* (1994), while Mario is holding his bike, he asks Neruda for a favor. What is it?
To write him a love poem so that he can woo the beautiful Beatrice.

In what movie did firefighter Tommy Corn ride his bicycle to a fire?
*I ♥ Huckabees* (2004).

True or False: *City Velo* is the name of the Pennsylvania-based magazine dedicated to bicycle culture in cities worldwide.
False. *Urban Velo.*

What US professional female cyclocross racer is best known for her vegan diet?
Christine "Peanut" Vardaros.

*Pure Sweet Hell* is a documentary focusing on which bicycle scene?
A. Cyclocross; B. Road; C. Track; D. Mountain bike
A. Cyclocross.

True or False: Radball (a German word literally translated as "wheel ball") is a sport similar to soccer, only the competitors play while riding bicycles.
True. The sport is also called Cycle Ball.

Schwinn BMX riders Jay Miron, Dave Osato and Joey Garcia all have pictures on the back of what famous cereal box?
Honey Nut Cheerios—thanks to Schwinn's sponsorship deal with them in 1997.

In 1963, a young Schwinn engineer named Al Fritz came up with a bike design (code named the J-38) that drew resistance from adults for being ugly but was instantly a success with kids. Hint: It came equipped with a banana seat.
Schwinn Sting-Ray, named after the winged creature of the sea.

What was the retail price of the above bike when it was first released?
A. 34.95; B. $49.95; C. $64.95; D. $74.95
B. $49.95. Schwinn sold over 40,000 Sting-Rays in 1963 alone. They would have sold more if the company hadn't run out of 20-inch tires.

The first true bicycle that was equipped with one big wheel and one small went under three names. Two of them are penny farthing and high wheel. What is the third?
Ordinary.

How did the penny farthing bicycle get its name?
From the British penny and farthing coins of that time, the former being much larger than the latter.

What was the size of the larger front wheel of a penny farthing?
A. 40 inches; B. 50 inches; C. 60 inches; D. 70 inches
C. 60 inches.

What is the name of the first magazine solely dedicated to all things cyclocross?
*Cyclo-Cross Magazine,* founded by Andrew Yee in 2007.

In what year did the Vienna Convention on Road Traffic of the United Nations consider a bicycle to be a vehicle, with the person controlling the bicycle considered a driver?
1968. The traffic codes of many countries were adjusted to reflect these definitions.

The bicycle craze in the 1890s led to a movement for so-called rational dress, which helped liberate women from corsets, ankle-length skirts, and what other famously popular yet restrictive garment?
Bloomers.

What is the name of the website that is world famous for listing actual versus published weights of bike parts?
Weightweenies.com.

What is the informational website most famous for its information on fixed-gear bikes? Hint: His trademark beard and plastic helmet-mounted eagle, named Igor, were matters of frequent comment.

SheldonBrown.com. Brown died from a heart attack on February 3, 2008 but the website remains.

What is the name of the bicycle taxi that originated in Africa in the 1960s?

Boda-Boda.

How did the bicycle taxi in question above get its name?

*Boda-boda* (border-to-border) was how the taxi drivers called out to potential customers. Its original purpose was to transport people across the Kenya-Uganda border to other regions. No paperwork was involved for those who crossed international borders on nonmotorized vehicles.

What is the name of the first vegan elite cycling team?

California-Based Organic Athlete Cycling Team.

To whom does this quote belong? "Let me tell you what I think of bicycling. I think it has done more to emancipate women than anything else in the world. It gives women a feeling of freedom and self-reliance. I stand and rejoice every time I see a woman ride by on a wheel . . . the picture of free, untrammeled womanhood."
A. Susan B. Anthony; B. Hillary Clinton; C. Walt Whitman; D. Erica Jong
A. Susan B. Anthony. She said it in a *New York World* interview on February 2, 1896

The 2000 documentary *The Bicycle Corps: America's Black Army on Wheels* depicted the 25th Infantry proving bicycles' practicality in the military in a rugged ride from Missoula, Montana, to St. Louis, in 1897. What bike did they use back then?
They were donated one-speed Spalding bikes. Each loaded bike weighed about 60 to 70 pounds.

In 1895 Frances Willard, the tightly laced president of the Women's Christian Temperance Union, wrote a powerfully influential book in which she used a cycling metaphor to urge other suffragists to action. What was the name of the book?
*How I Learned to Ride the Bicycle*, in which she praised the bicycle she learned to ride late in life, which she named Gladys, for its "gladdening effect" on her health and political optimism.

Which 2001 niche film about women cyclists featured Jacquie Phelan as guide?
*HardiHood.*

True or False: In *The Cyclist,* a 1987 film directed by Mohsen Makhmalbaf, Nasim, an Afghan well digger in Iran, raises money for his wife's medical treatment by riding his bike around a vacant lot for three days and nights without stopping.
False. It was seven days. Nasim was a former champion three-day bicycle marathoner.

The Flying Scotsman Graeme Obree broke the world hour record in 1993 on a bike he designed and built himself. What did he lovingly refer to it as?
Old Faithful.

What is the name of the movie that begins with this statement? "Good news. The bustle is in its decline, allowing for the meteoric rise of that newfangled creation, the bicycle."
William Shakespeare's *A Midsummer Night's Dream* (1999).

Which 1994 movie set in New York City is a remake of the 1948 Italian neo-realist classic, *The Bicycle Thief?*
*Messenger.* Written and directed by Norman Loftis.

What is the name of the Italian film where the protaganist's bike frames the entire film, literally and figuratively? Hint: Many scenes are filmed through a bike wheel.
*Malèna* (2000).

What is the date of International Car Free Day?
A. January 1; B. June 12; C. August 25; D. September 22
D. September 22.

True or False: In the 2005 documentary *Wired to Win: Surviving the Tour de France*, Australian sprinter Baden Cooke suffers an injury early in the race, providing the filmmakers with an ideal opportunity to connect his recovery and return to the race with the science behind his motivation.
False. It was his teammate, French cyclist, Jimmy Caspar.

The documentary *Wired to Win: Surviving the Tour de France* uses what year of the Tour de France as its backdrop?
2003.

True or False: In the classic Italian film, *The Bicycle Thief* (1948), as Ricci is riding to his first day of his new job of hanging posters, his bike is stolen.
True.

Critical Mass originated in what city?
A. San Francisco; B. New York City; C. Chicago; D. Los Angeles
A. San Francisco

What year was Critical Mass started?
A. 1979; B. 1988; C. 1992; D. 1996
C. September 25, 1992.

True or False: The original name of Critical Mass was Commute Clot.
True.

E-V Sunny Bicycle, the first all-solar electric bicycle driven completely from power derived from the sun's rays, weighs how many pounds?
A. 35 pounds; B. 50 pounds; C. 75 pounds; D. 90 pounds
C. 75 pounds.

True or False: A bicycle saddle is also known as a bicycle seat.
False. A bicycle seat, unlike a saddle, is designed to support 100% of the rider's weight and is found attached to a recumbent bicycle.

In what year was the membership level highest for the League of American Bicyclists (LAB), a nonprofit organization promoting cycling for fun, fitness, and transportation through advocacy and education?
A. 1898; B. 1951; C. 1978; D. 2005
A. 1898. Membership peaked at 103,000.

Which county's Safe Routes to Schools Program received a prestigious 2003 Award for Public Service from the National Highway Traffic Safety Administration (NHTSA)?
Marin County in California.

What is a ghost bike?
A junker bike that has been painted white and affixed to the site where a cyclist has been hit or killed by a car.

True or False: Foot Down is a contest where the winner is the last person still riding the bike.
True. This race is also known as Bike Derby.

What is the name of the yearly multiple-day event held in the Nevada desert where beach cruisers are common?
Burning Man.

True or False: Bike polo is played with singlespeed bikes.
False. Fixed-gear bikes are used.

The Italian Classic film *The Bicycle Thief* (1948) is set in which city?
Rome.

In a scene of the 2005 film *Rent*, what was piled into a sculpture that served as a backdrop for a scene with a homeless woman?
Bike parts.

In the *Rent,* what does lead character Mark have mounted on his handlebar?
A small movie camera.

In the film *Rushmore* (1998), Max and Blume are at odds when they have both fallen for the same teacher. Max attacks Blume with a hive of bees; but how does Blume retaliate?
He runs over Max's beloved bicycle with his car.

In the documentary *Emmanuel's Gift* (2005), narrated by Oprah Winfrey, Emmanuel rides 380 miles across Ghana with a severely deformed leg on a bike supplied by what organization?
Challenged Athletes Foundation (CAF).

In the 2004 Tour de France documentary *Hell on Wheels*, which one of the racers ponders out loud, "Why didn't I become a surfer"?
A. Erik Zabel; B. Rolf Aldag; C. Andreas Klöden; D. Jan Ullrich
A. Erik Zabel

True or False: The movies *Il Postino, Beijing Bicycle, 40-Year-Old Virgin,* and *City of God* all portray the bicycle as a key means of survival in impoverished societies.
False. *40-Year-Old Virgin* does not.

In the documentary *Go Further* (2003) starring Woody Harrelson, what controversial act is done to the American flag?
It's hung upside-down on a bike.

In the 1997 Roberto Benigni film *Life is Beautiful* (*La Vita è Bella*), there are two scenes in which the lead protagonist is riding a bike. What are they?
In one scene, Guido grabs a bicycle to escape a pompous, heartless bureaucrat with whom he has had an altercation; it leads him literally into the arms of Dora, whom he is courting. The second scene comes at the end of the film: Guido rides his wife and son through the busy streets of town to work and then to school.

In what year and what city was Campagnolo founded?
1933 in Vicenza.

What was the color of Guo's trusty steed in the 2001 film *Beijing Bicycle?*
A. Red; B. White; C. Black; D. silver
Silver.

*The Middle of the World* (2003) is a story about a family's quest to find a better life by relocating on bicycle from poverty-ridden Paraiba, Brazil, to what major city?
Rio de Janeiro.

In the 1984 film *The Karate Kid,* where does Daniel's bike first appear?
In the first scene of the movie, on the roof of his mother's car as they pull out of the driveway to move from Newark, New Jersey, to Reseda, California.

What is the name of the 1999 documentary about three friends who bike from Venice Beach, California, to Springfield, Massachusetts, to visit the National Basketball Association's Hall of Fame?
*True Fans.*

In which Jim Carrey movie did his wife ride a bike?
A. *Liar Liar*; B. *The Truman Show*; C. *Man on the Moon*; D. *Bruce Almighty*
B. *The Truman Show* (1998).

In the movie *40-Year-Old Virgin*, what type of truck did Andy run into in the bike-car chase scene?
Billboard truck.

True or False: When Andy crashed into the truck in *40-Year-Old Virgin*, he was not wearing a helmet.
False.

What type of bike is common in an alley-cat race?
A. BMX; B. Mountain bike; C. Track bike; D. Cyclocross
C. A fixed-gear or track bike.

What mojo is found on Pee-Wee's bicycle handlebar in the 1985 film *Pee-Wee's Big Adventure*?
A tiger head

Professional cycling legend Johan Museeuw is now producing frames made of carbon mixed with what natural fiber?
Flax.

What custom framebuilder is responsible for making the Wise-Cracker Bottle Opener, made specifically to mount on seat tubes, steerer tubes, or shop stands?
A. Seven Cycles; B. Ahrens Bicycles; C. Sycip; D. WTB
B. Ahrens Bicycles.

Which event does not exist?
A. Bike to Work Day; B. Bike to Work Week; C. Bike to Work Month; D. They all exist
D. They all exist.

The soundtrack from Francis Ford Coppola's movie *One from the Heart* included a song about bicycles. What was that song?
"Broken Bicycles" written by multiple Grammy Award winner Tom Waits; the soundtrack was nominated for an Academy Award.

What is the slang name for a fixed-gear bike?
Fixie.

True or False: Urban Bike Polo is traditional bike polo played on pavement instead of grass.
True. It is also referred to as Urban Cycle Polo.

What is the derisive term used by cyclists to describe another cyclist, usually male, who appears amateurish and oblivious to cycling culture?
A Fred.

What is the name of the Minneapolis-based company that equates cars with coffins?
Cars-R-Coffins.

A single-ended socket wrench with a flat handle commonly used for tightening crank fixing bolts and track nuts is often referred to what popular cyclist sandwich spread?
Peanut Butter Wrench. While on the road, racers use the handle of this wrench to spread peanut butter on their bread.

True or False: There exists an annual bicycle race called Tour de Donut where racers' final times are reduced by 5 minutes for each donut they consume along the way.
True. This 30-mile race is held in Staunton, Illinois.